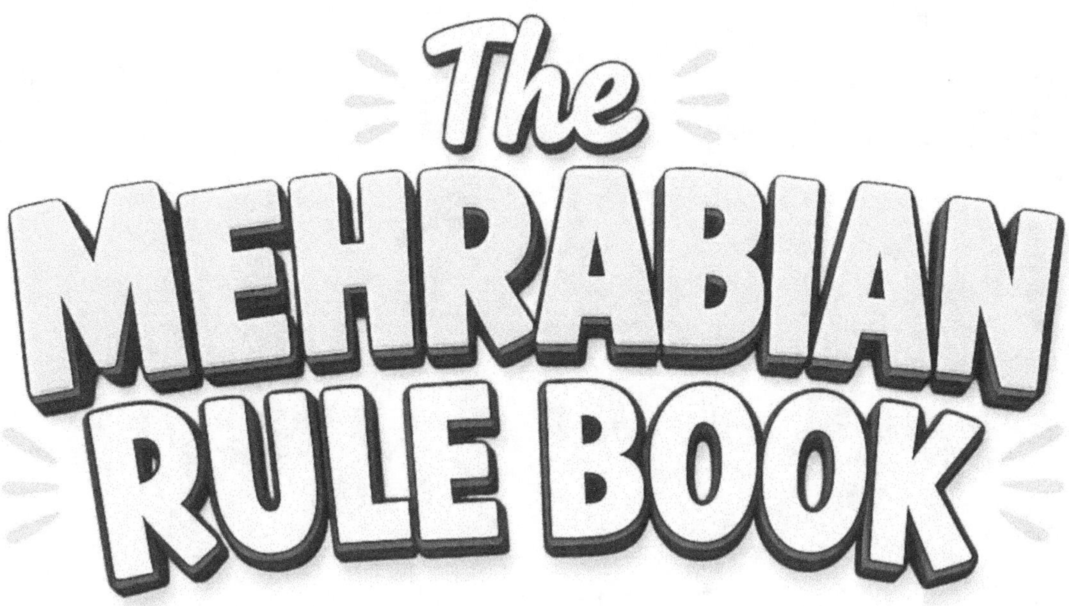

Helping Kids Read People, Understand Emotions, and Communicate with Confidence in Everyday Situations

Matthew Nobis

Copyright

This book is intended for educational and personal growth purposes only. It is not a substitute for professional psychological, medical, therapeutic, or counseling advice. If you or someone you know is experiencing serious emotional distress, bullying, anxiety, or mental health concerns, please seek support from a trusted adult or qualified professional.

The examples, names, characters, and situations in this book are fictional or used for illustrative purposes. Any resemblance to actual persons, schools, or events is purely coincidental.

TABLE OF CONTENTS

Everything in this book is about the invisible signals that shape every conversation.

INTRODUCTION — The Invisible Signals Everyone Misses 4

Something Felt Off ... 4
People Speak Before They Talk ... 5
The Rule Hidden Inside Human Communication ... 6
Why Words Are Only Part of the Story ... 7
Your Brain Is Watching Everything ... 8
The Social Skill Most People Never Learn ... 9
What Happens When You Finally Start Seeing the Signals ... 10

PART I — THE SECRET LANGUAGE PEOPLE USE 11

Your Face Speaks Before You Do ... 12
Why "I'm Fine" Doesn't Always Mean Fine ... 14
The Voice Behind the Words ... 16
What a Smile Can Really Mean ... 18
The Hidden Messages in Body Language ... 20
When Words, Voice, and Feelings Don't Match ... 22

PART II — THE SIGNALS YOU SEND WITHOUT KNOWING 24

The Face You Make When You Feel Nervous ... 25
Why Crossing Your Arms Changes Everything ... 27
Looking Confident Even When You Feel Scared ... 29
The Difference Between Calm and Weak ... 31
The Energy You Bring Into a Room ... 33
Why People Copy Each Other Without Realizing ... 35

PART III — SCHOOL IS FULL OF SIGNALS 37

Reading the Classroom Mood ... 38
When the Teacher Is Actually Annoyed ... 40
Group Projects and Silent Drama ... 42
The Invisible Rules of the Lunch Table ... 44
Knowing When to Speak Up ... 46
The Fastest Way to Lose a Room ... 48

PART IV — FRIENDSHIP CAN GET CONFUSING 50

"I Was Kidding" — Or Was I? ... 51
Real Laughs vs. Fake Laughs ... 53
When a Friend Starts Pulling Away ... 55
Being Included vs. Being Tolerated ... 57
The Friend Who Changes Around Other People ... 59
The Joke Everyone Understands Except You ... 61

PART V — THE HIDDEN RULES OF GROUPS 63

Why Groups Sometimes Exclude Someone ... 64
The Leader Everyone Quietly Follows ... 66
The Kid Who Controls the Mood ... 68
Feeling Invisible in a Group ... 70
Spotting Fake Confidence ... 72
Why People Act Different Around Friends ... 74

PART VI — TOUGH MOMENTS & SOCIAL PRESSURE 76

The Silence That Feels Heavy ... 77
Calm Voices That Aren't Calm ... 79
When Someone Wants a Reaction From You ... 81
Teasing, Joking, or Bullying? ... 83
Standing Your Ground Without Starting a Fight ... 85
How to Tell When Someone Feels Uncomfortable ... 87

PART VII — BECOMING SOMEONE PEOPLE TRUST 89

Listening So People Feel Heard ... 90
The Body Language of Leadership ... 92
The Power of Making Others Feel Safe ... 94
Saying Sorry So People Believe You ... 96
Telling the Truth Clearly ... 98
Making Your Words, Voice, and Actions Match ... 100

PART VIII — TRY THIS IN REAL LIFE 102

The No-Word Challenge ... 103
Watch a Movie With the Sound Off ... 105
Guess the Real Emotion ... 107
The Mirror Exercise ... 109
Reading Text Messages Like a Detective ... 111
The Skill Most Adults Never Learn ... 113

BONUS SECTION 115

Social Signal Quiz ... 115
Decode the Expression Game ... 118
Real-Life Communication Challenges ... 120
Certificate of Observation Skills ... 122

INTRODUCTION —

The Invisible Signals Everyone Misses

Something Felt Off

Ethan stepped into the classroom and immediately felt it.

Nobody said anything strange. Nobody pointed at him. The teacher was still writing on the board. A few kids were talking near the windows like they always did before class started.

But something felt different.

One conversation suddenly became quieter. A girl looked at him for half a second before quickly turning back toward her friend. Somebody gave a short laugh that seemed to stop too fast. Even the air in the room somehow felt tense, like Ethan had walked into the middle of something he was not fully supposed to see.

By the time he sat down, his stomach already felt tight.

The strange part was that he could not explain why.

• • •

This happens to people constantly. You walk into a room and instantly feel comfortable... or uncomfortable. Sometimes a teacher says "good morning," but you can already tell they are stressed. Sometimes a friend claims nothing is wrong while clearly acting different. Other times a group of people suddenly feels awkward the second one person arrives.

Most people think these feelings are random.

They are not.

Human beings are constantly sending signals to each other without realizing it. Tiny facial expressions. Changes in tone. Body language. Eye contact. Energy shifts inside a group. Your brain notices these clues automatically, even when you are not consciously trying to analyze anybody.

That is why social situations can sometimes feel exhausting or confusing. Your brain is processing far more information than just words. In fact, many conversations begin emotionally long before anyone actually starts talking.

People are emotional observers by nature.

Adults experience this too, even if they pretend they do not.

A parent can tell their child is upset from the way they walk through the front door.

A coach can sense nervousness before a big game without hearing a single sentence.

Teachers often know when tension is building in a classroom before students say anything out loud.

The strange thing is that almost nobody explains how this invisible social world actually works.

Kids are expected to "read the room." They are expected to notice when somebody feels uncomfortable, annoyed, sarcastic, nervous, fake, embarrassed, left out, or angry.

But nobody really teaches them how.

Most of those answers live inside signals people barely notice consciously.

- A voice becoming colder.
- A smile disappearing too quickly.
- Someone crossing their arms during a conversation.
- A tiny glance between two friends.
- A long pause before answering.

None of these things seem important alone.
But together, they create emotional messages that people react to automatically every single day.

And once you begin noticing these invisible signals, the social world starts making a lot more sense.

You realize maybe people were communicating the entire time.
Just not with words alone.

People Speak Before They Talk

Imagine somebody smiling at you while saying, "Nice to see you." Now imagine the exact same words spoken with crossed arms, a flat voice, and eyes that immediately look away.

The sentence stayed the same.
But the feeling changed completely.

That is because communication is not only about words. Long before people carefully think about what they want to say, their face, tone, posture, and energy are already sending signals to everybody around them.

In other words, people often speak before they actually talk.

This happens so fast that most humans do not even realize they are doing it. The brain constantly scans other people for emotional clues. Are they safe? Nervous? Friendly? Annoyed? Confident? Fake? Uncomfortable? Excited? Bored? Your mind quietly searches for answers almost every second during social situations.

That is why you can sometimes tell a teacher is stressed before class even begins. It is why certain classmates seem intimidating without openly saying anything mean. It is why one person can make a room feel relaxed while another somehow creates tension immediately.

Words matter.
But they are only part of the message.

Imagine a friend saying:

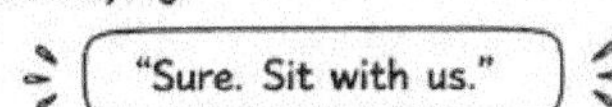

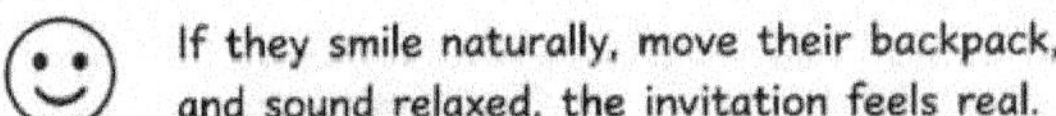

If they smile naturally, move their backpack, and sound relaxed, the invitation feels real.

But if they avoid eye contact, keep their arms crossed, and answer with a cold voice, the exact same sentence suddenly feels completely different.

Most people react more strongly to the emotional signals surrounding words than to the words themselves. Human beings trust feelings faster than language. That is one reason arguments sometimes begin even when technically "nothing bad was said." Somebody reacts to the tone. Or the expression. Or the energy underneath the sentence.

Adults do this constantly too.
"You seem upset."
"I said I'm fine."
"Yes, but you don't sound fine."

People say things like this every day because emotionally, humans understand that communication includes much more than vocabulary alone.

This invisible social language is happening everywhere:

- in classrooms
- during friendships
- at family dinners
- during group projects
- in sports
- online calls
- even during silence

Sometimes silence itself communicates something powerful. A heavy silence feels different from a comfortable silence. A quick pause before answering can completely change the mood of a conversation. Even the speed somebody responds can reveal emotion.

Think about how different these answers feel:

"Okay!" "Okay..." "Okay."

Same word.
Completely different emotional message.

Most people never consciously study these hidden signals. They simply react to them automatically their entire lives. But once you begin noticing them, human behavior suddenly becomes much easier to understand.

You realize people are constantly showing emotions before they fully explain them.

- A nervous person may laugh too quickly.
- Someone embarrassed may suddenly become quieter.
- A confident person may stay calm while everybody else gets louder.
- Another person may pretend not to care while their face reveals disappointment immediately.

None of this means you should obsess over every little movement people make. Humans are complicated. One expression or tone alone does not always tell the whole story. The important thing is learning to notice patterns instead of only listening to words.

Because the truth is, communication starts long before sentences do. And once you understand that, the social world stops feeling quite so random.

The Rule Hidden Inside Human Communication

For a long time, scientists believed communication was mostly about words.

Say the right thing.

Use the correct sentence.

Choose good answers.

But then a psychology professor named Albert Mehrabian studied something interesting: what happens when a person's words do not match their emotions.

For example, imagine somebody saying:

"I'm really happy to see you."

But their voice sounds cold.
And their face looks annoyed.

What do people believe?

The words?
Or the emotion underneath them?

Most people trust the emotion.

That is where the famous Mehrabian Rule comes from.

The rule is often explained like this:

When emotions and words do not match:

- ★ words communicate part of the message
- ★ tone of voice communicates a bigger part
- ★ facial expressions and body language communicate the biggest part

This idea later became known as the "7–38–55 Rule."

The numbers are usually explained this way:

7% = words

38% = tone of voice

55% = facial expressions and body language

Now, this does NOT mean words are unimportant. Words matter a lot. If somebody gives directions, explains homework, or tells a story, the actual language is obviously important.

But the Mehrabian Rule reveals something fascinating about emotions:
People often believe feelings more than sentences.

That is why somebody can technically say something nice while still sounding rude.
It is why a fake apology feels fake immediately.
It is why one teacher can calm an entire classroom just by the way they speak, while another creates stress before anybody even understands why.

Humans are emotional readers.
We constantly search each other for clues about what people truly feel underneath their words.

Imagine semobody saying:

"Good luck today."

If they smile warmly and sound encouraging, the sentence feels supportive.

But if they roll their eyes and say it sarcastically, the exact same words suddenly feel insulting.

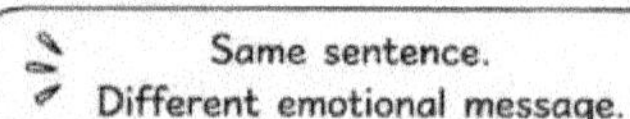

Same sentence.
Different emotional message.

That is the hidden rule inside human communication.
People are always reacting to:

- facial expressions
- tone
- posture
- energy
- timing
- eye contact
- emotional consistency

When all those signals match together, communication feels honest and clear. But when they clash, conversations suddenly feel uncomfortable, awkward, fake, tense, or confusing.

You have probably experienced this already without realizing it.

- ★ Maybe a friend said "it's okay" while clearly looking upset.
- ★ Maybe somebody laughed during a conversation even though they seemed uncomfortable.
- ★ Maybe you could instantly tell a parent was stressed before they said a single word.

Your brain was already reading emotional signals.

That is what makes the Mehrabian Rule so interesting.
It explains something humans do naturally every single day but rarely think about consciously.

People are constantly communicating emotions without fully realizing it.
And once you understand this, a lot of social situations suddenly start making more sense.

You stop focusing only on the words people say.
You start noticing the full message instead.

The voice.

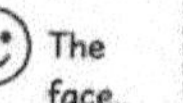

The face.

The body.

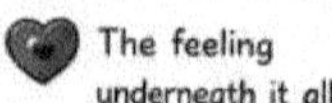

The feeling underneath it all.

That is the invisible language this entire book is about.

Why Words Are Only Part of the Story

Two students can say the exact same sentence and create completely different feelings.

"Nice shot."

One says it while smiling naturally and sounding impressed.
The other says it with a smirk and a sarcastic voice while looking at their friends afterward.

Same words.
Different message.

This is something many people do not fully realize at first: words are only one piece of communication. Human beings are constantly reacting to the emotion surrounding the sentence, not just the sentence itself.

That is why certain conversations feel comfortable immediately while others feel tense even when nobody technically says anything rude.

Imagine somebody saying:

"Whatever."

Depending on the tone, expression, and body language, that single word could mean:

- "I honestly don't care."
- "I'm annoyed."
- "I'm hurt."
- "I'm trying to act cool."
- "I want this conversation to end."

The word alone does not explain the real feeling.
The **emotional signals around it** do.

This happens because human communication is **deeply emotional**. Your brain constantly tries to answer hidden questions during conversations:

- Does this person seem genuine?
- Do they actually mean what they are saying?
- Are they uncomfortable?
- Nervous?
- Friendly?
- Defensive?
- Safe to trust?

Most of this happens automatically without conscious effort.

That is why people can often "feel" tension before understanding it logically. A group project may suddenly become awkward even though everybody is still being polite. A family dinner may feel uncomfortable long before an argument officially starts. A classroom can instantly change mood the second a frustrated teacher walks in.

Words alone rarely create those feelings.
The **emotional signals underneath** them do.

Think about how different these two moments feel:

✓ A friend quietly says, "Are you okay?" while genuinely looking concerned.

✗ Another person says the exact same sentence while laughing and clearly making fun of somebody.

Same words.
Completely different emotional experience.

Adults struggle with this constantly too. Sometimes people focus only on the sentence itself and ignore the emotion underneath it.

"I was joking." → "Then why did it sound mean?"
"I said I was fine." → "You didn't look fine."

Conversations like this happen every single day because humans naturally react to more than language. Tone of voice, expressions, timing, posture, energy, and eye contact all shape the meaning of what somebody says.

This is also why texting can create misunderstandings so easily. Online, people lose many emotional clues. A short message may accidentally sound angry when the person typing it was actually relaxed. A joke may sound rude without facial expressions or tone helping explain it.

Real-life communication contains layers.
Words are only one layer.
Underneath them, there is another invisible conversation happening constantly through emotion and behavior.

Once you begin noticing this, social situations stop feeling quite so random. You start understanding why some people seem trustworthy instantly while others feel fake even when they say all the "right" things. You notice why some apologies feel real and others feel forced. You begin seeing why certain friendships feel emotionally safe while others feel exhausting.

☆ And maybe most importantly, you realize something powerful:

If communication is more than words...
then understanding people is more than listening.

It is observing the full story people are telling without realizing it.

Your Brain Is Watching Everything

Have you ever met somebody and instantly felt comfortable around them? Or uncomfortable?

Sometimes it happens before the person has even finished introducing themselves. Your brain reacts first, and only later do you try explaining the feeling with words.

That is because the human brain is constantly observing people, even when you are not consciously trying to analyze anyone.

Your mind notices:

- Facial expressions.
- Tone changes.
-  Body language.
-  Movement.
-  Energy shifts inside groups.
-  Tiny pauses.
-  Quick glances between people.

Most of this happens automatically and incredibly fast.

In fact, scientists believe the brain processes emotional signals before we fully think about them logically. That is why social situations can sometimes feel exhausting without you understanding exactly why. Your brain is collecting information nonstop the entire time.

Imagine walking into a classroom where everybody suddenly goes quiet.

Nobody says:

"We were talking about you."

But your brain immediately pays attention.

Or imagine asking a question while somebody gives a quick glance to their friend before answering. Technically, nothing important happened. But somehow the interaction suddenly feels different.
Your brain noticed the signal.

Humans evolved this way for a reason. Long ago, paying attention to emotional and social clues helped people stay safe, build trust, avoid danger, and survive in groups. Even now, your brain constantly asks hidden questions during conversations:

- Does this person seem safe?
- Friendly?
- Nervous?
- Angry?
- Honest?
- Fake?
- Comfortable around me?

Most people never consciously hear these questions in their minds. But the brain is still searching for answers anyway.

That is why some people can "read the room" quickly. They are noticing emotional patterns happening around them, often without realizing how much information their brain is collecting automatically.

You have probably experienced this many times already.

- Maybe a teacher walked into class in a perfectly normal mood, but everybody instantly relaxed anyway.
- Maybe somebody said "don't worry about it" while clearly looking upset.
- Maybe you could feel tension building between two friends before they actually started arguing.

Your brain was already reading signals.

This is also why emotions spread through groups so easily.
One nervous person can make everybody else tense.
One confident person can calm an entire team.
One awkward moment can suddenly change the energy of a lunch table or classroom.
Humans constantly affect each other emotionally.
Even silently.

And the strange part is that many people think social confidence means talking more, acting louder, or saying the perfect thing. But socially aware people often do something much more important first:

They observe.

They notice.

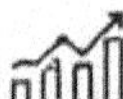

They pay attention to patterns.

Because people reveal far more than they realize.

A student pretending to act confident may keep checking whether others are laughing at them. Someone acting "fine" may suddenly become quieter than usual. A person trying to hide embarrassment may smile too quickly or avoid eye contact for half a second.

Most of these signals happen automatically.
Your brain notices many of them before you consciously understand what feels strange.

That does not mean you should become paranoid or overthink every interaction. Human beings are complicated. One signal alone rarely explains everything. The important thing is learning that social situations are full of invisible information most people ignore completely.

Once you understand this, the world starts feeling different.
You stop seeing conversations as only words.
You begin seeing emotions, reactions, tension, confidence, nervousness, and hidden feelings moving underneath the surface all the time.

And maybe that is why certain moments feel so powerful even when almost nothing was actually said.
Your brain was watching the entire conversation long before the words finished.

The Social Skill Most People Never Learn

Most schools teach math. Reading. Science. History.
But almost nobody teaches kids how people actually work.

Nobody sits down and explains why one group feels welcoming while another feels uncomfortable. Nobody explains why certain people seem instantly trustworthy while others somehow make everybody tense. Nobody explains why a simple sentence can sound kind, sarcastic, awkward, fake, nervous, or confident depending on the face and tone attached to it.

And yet people deal with these invisible social situations every single day.
At school. At lunch. During sports. Inside friendships. During arguments. In group chats. At family dinners.

Almost every important moment between humans depends on communication far beyond words alone.

That is why social misunderstandings happen constantly. One person believes they were "just joking." Another person feels embarrassed or hurt. Somebody thinks they sounded calm while actually sounding angry. Another person says "I don't care" while secretly hoping somebody notices they are upset.

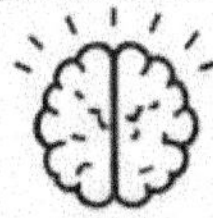

Most people move through social situations without fully understanding the signals they are sending or receiving.

The strange part is that socially skilled people are not always the loudest, funniest, or most popular people in the room.

Very often, they are simply the people who notice more.

- ★ They notice tension early.
- ★ They notice discomfort before it becomes conflict.
- ★ They notice when somebody feels left out.
- ★ They notice when words and emotions do not match.
- ★ They notice the mood of a room changing before everybody else does.

That is a real skill.
And surprisingly, many adults never fully develop it.

Some people grow up still misunderstanding tone.
Still missing sarcasm. Still ignoring body language. Still believing communication is only about the literal sentence being spoken.

That is one reason social situations can sometimes feel exhausting or confusing. People are reacting to invisible emotional signals constantly, even when nobody explains the rules out loud.

Think about how often people say things like:

- "Read the room."
- "That sounded rude."
- "You can tell she's uncomfortable."
- "Something feels off."
- "He clearly didn't mean it."

All of those reactions come from reading **emotional signals** underneath words.

The problem is that many kids secretly believe there is something wrong with them when social situations feel hard to understand.

But often, nobody ever explained the hidden patterns in the first place.

Nobody explained that people communicate through:

- tone
- expressions
- posture
- timing
- energy
- pauses
- eye contact
- emotional consistency

Nobody explained that groups have invisible rules.
That confidence changes body language.
That nervousness changes tone.
That fake smiles feel different from real ones.
That silence itself can communicate emotion.

Once you begin understanding these patterns, something interesting happens.

People stop seeming completely random.

- ✓ You begin understanding why certain conversations feel awkward.
- ✓ Why some people seem emotionally safe.
- ✓ Why tension spreads through groups.
- ✓ Why one person can calm an entire room while another creates discomfort without saying much at all.

And maybe most importantly, you begin understanding yourself better too.

You realize social confidence is not about becoming fake, manipulative, or perfect.
It is not about memorizing tricks or pretending to be somebody else.

Real social awareness is much simpler than that.

It is learning to notice what is already happening around you.

Because the truth is, humans are constantly communicating invisible emotional information all the time.
Most people just never learn how to see it clearly.

 **That is the skill this book is really about.** 

What Happens When You Finally Start Seeing the Signals

At first, nothing changes.

 People still joke around at lunch.

 Teachers still give homework.

 Friends still text weird replies that make no sense.

 The world looks exactly the same.

But then you begin noticing things you never saw before.

You notice the student who acts loud whenever they feel insecure. You notice how certain people suddenly change personality depending on who is around them. You notice fake laughs. Nervous smiles. Tension inside group projects before arguments even begin.

 You start realizing that social situations are full of invisible emotional conversations happening underneath the words.

And once you see those patterns, it becomes difficult to unsee them.

- ★ Movies become more interesting.
- ★ Friendships start making more sense.
- ★ You notice when somebody wants attention, when somebody feels left out, or when somebody is pretending not to care.
- ★ You begin understanding why certain classmates feel emotionally safe while others somehow make everybody uncomfortable without openly doing anything wrong.

You also begin understanding yourself differently.

 Maybe you realize you are not "bad at people."

 Maybe you were simply noticing signals other people ignored.

 Or maybe nobody ever explained the hidden rules clearly before.

 That realization changes something important.
It makes the social world feel less random.
Less mysterious.
Less scary.

A lot of kids secretly believe social confidence means:

- ✕ always knowing what to say
- ✕ never feeling awkward
- ✕ acting fearless
- ✕ being loud or funny
- ✕ becoming popular instantly

Real social awareness usually looks much quieter than that.

 It looks like noticing when somebody feels uncomfortable.

 It looks like understanding tone before reacting emotionally.

 It looks like realizing that some arguments are not really about the words at all.

 It looks like recognizing when a friend is trying to hide embarrassment instead of immediately assuming they are angry or rude.

 Socially aware people are often better observers, not better performers.
That is an important difference.

 Because this book is not about becoming fake or learning manipulation tricks. It is not about controlling people or acting like a human lie detector. Real communication is more complicated than that.

 Human beings are messy.
Sometimes people send mixed signals accidentally.
Sometimes they say things they do not fully mean.
Sometimes nervousness looks like anger.
Sometimes embarrassment sounds sarcastic.
Sometimes people smile while feeling hurt because they do not want others noticing.

 Learning to see social signals is not about judging people instantly.
It is about understanding them more clearly.

And strangely, the more you understand people, the less confusing many social situations become.

- ✓ You stop taking every awkward moment personally.
- ✓ You stop assuming every strange reaction means somebody hates you.
- ✓ You begin realizing that other people are often confused, nervous, insecure, emotional, and uncertain too — even when they pretend otherwise.

 **And maybe that is the biggest hidden secret behind communication: Most people are walking around trying to understand each other while barely realizing how much they are already saying without words.** →

 Once you finally start seeing the signals, you begin understanding the invisible emotional world people create around themselves every single day.

 And after that, conversations never quite look the same again. 

PART I

THE SECRET LANGUAGE PEOPLE USE

Most people think communication starts with words.
It doesn't.

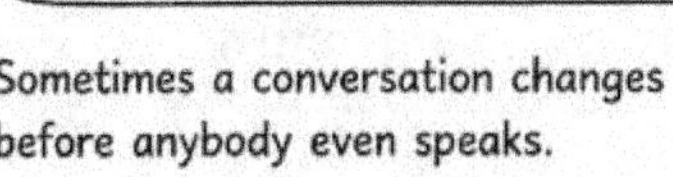

Sometimes a conversation changes before anybody even speaks.

- ★ A face tightens for half a second.
- ★ Someone looks away too quickly.
- ★ A smile appears... but disappears almost instantly.

And somehow, your brain notices.

That is the strange thing about people:
we are constantly sending signals without realizing it.

 Tiny emotional clues.

 Tiny reactions.

 Tiny changes in tone, posture, timing, and expression.

Most adults notice these signals automatically...
without ever understanding how they learned them.
That's why social situations can feel confusing sometimes.

You may walk into a room and instantly feel:
something is off.
Even if nobody says anything directly.

You may hear:
"I'm fine."
But somehow know the person is not actually fine.

You may trust one person immediately...

and feel uncomfortable around another...

without fully understanding why.

This section is about those invisible signals.
The hidden language underneath conversations.

Because people communicate through much more than words alone.

They communicate through:

 facial expressions 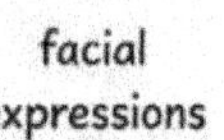	 voice changes	 eye contact
 body language	 timing	 emotional energy

And once you start noticing these patterns...
you begin understanding people in a completely different way.

Not in a creepy "mind-reading" way.
More like finally seeing the hidden rules that were always there.

The goal is not to judge people.
And it is definitely not about becoming fake.
It is about awareness.

Because when you understand the signals people send...
you also start understanding yourself better.

You notice:

- ★ why certain rooms feel tense
- ★ why some people feel safe instantly
- ★ why fake smiles feel different than real ones
- ★ why some conversations drain your energy
- ★ why certain people can change the mood of an entire group

A lot of kids secretly believe:
"Maybe I'm bad at people."
But often...
nobody ever explained how the invisible social world actually works.

This section will help you start seeing it.
The secret language people use every single day –
without realizing they are speaking it.

Your Face Speaks Before You Do

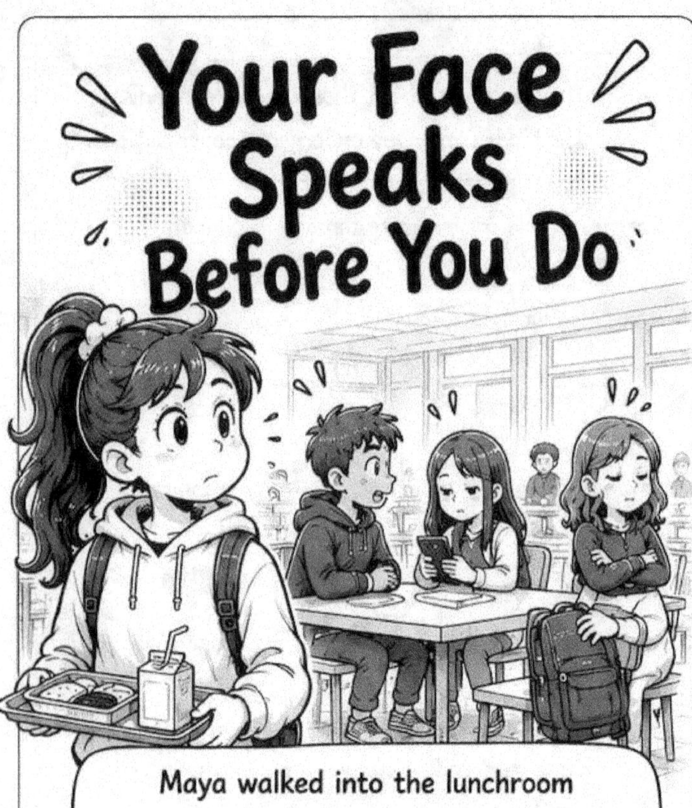

Maya walked into the lunchroom carrying her tray and instantly felt something was off.

- ★ Nobody said anything strange.
- ★ But two kids suddenly stopped talking.
- ★ One girl looked down at her phone too fast.
- ★ Another gave a tiny smile that disappeared almost immediately.
- ★ A boy moved his backpack onto the empty chair beside him without even looking up.

Maya had the strange feeling that the room had already decided something before she even sat down.

That is the weird thing about people. Sometimes a room speaks before anybody says a word.

Most people think communication starts when someone opens their mouth. But humans are already reading faces long before words arrive.

A raised eyebrow.

Tight lips.

Eyes that suddenly look away.

A smile that feels real.

Another that lasts half a second too long.

Your brain notices these things automatically.

Even when you do not realize it.

That is why you can sometimes tell a teacher is annoyed before they say anything. Or why a friend can say "I'm fine" while somehow looking completely not fine at all.

Faces leak emotions constantly. Not perfectly. But constantly.

A person may try to sound relaxed while their expression looks nervous.

Someone may laugh while secretly feeling uncomfortable.

Another person may act confident while their face keeps checking whether other people approve of them.

Most of the time, people are sending emotional signals without realizing it. And other people are picking them up without realizing it too.

That is one reason social situations can feel confusing.

Your brain reacts to signals before your mind fully explains them.

Sometimes you suddenly feel awkward, nervous, safe, included, ignored, or uncomfortable — and only later realize your brain was reacting to facial expressions, tone, and body language the entire time.

awkward

nervous

safe

included

ignored

uncomfortable

Signals to Notice

Here are a few facial signals people often notice without thinking about it:

- smiles that disappear very quickly

- eyebrows tightening for a second

- eyes rolling upward

- lips pressed together before answering

- someone avoiding eye contact after saying something

- fake-looking smiles that never reach the eyes

One signal alone does not always mean something important.
But patterns usually do.

Real-Life Example

During group project time, Ethan asked if he could join a table near the window.

★ The word sounded friendly.

★ But nobody moved over.

★ Nobody looked at him.

★ One boy exchanged a fast glance with another boy before going back to his paper.

Ethan suddenly felt like he was interrupting something.
Nothing openly rude had happened.
But the faces at the table were already sending a message.

This happens constantly in everyday life. People often believe communication is only about words, but expressions quietly change the meaning of everything. The exact same sentence can feel warm, cold, awkward, sarcastic, welcoming, or angry depending on the face attached to it.

Think about how different this sounds depending on the expression:

"Nice job." → One person smiles naturally while saying it.

"Nice job." → Another says the exact same words while smirking and rolling their eyes.

Same sentence.
Completely different feeling.

That is because faces help carry emotion. In many situations, expressions communicate feelings faster than language does.

And once you notice this, the social world starts making a lot more sense.

You begin understanding:

why some people feel trustworthy instantly.

why certain classmates make everybody nervous without saying much.

why some teachers calm a room just by walking in.

why some smiles feel safe and others feel fake.

You also begin noticing something important about yourself:

Sometimes you think you are hiding nervousness while your expression is giving it away immediately.

Sometimes you believe you sound calm while your face looks irritated or embarrassed.

People are constantly reading each other's emotional clues.

Most adults never consciously learn this.
They just react to it automatically.

Try This

Today, quietly observe people's expressions for a few minutes.
Not in a creepy way.
Just pay attention.

Notice:

- what real excitement looks like
- what nervousness looks like
- how fast fake smiles disappear
- what happens to people's faces when they feel left out
- how expressions change before someone speaks

You will probably notice something surprising.
Very often, a face tells the story first.
The words arrive later

Why "I'm Fine" Doesn't Always Mean Fine

- Lena said it while staring down at her shoes.
- Her voice sounded flat.
- Her shoulders looked tight.
- She kept pulling at the sleeve of her hoodie instead of looking at her friend.
- But technically, the words sounded completely normal.

That happens all the time with people. **Sometimes words tell one story while the rest of the person tells another.**

A person may say they are okay while looking upset. Someone may claim they are not nervous while bouncing their leg nonstop under the table. Another person may loudly insist they "do not care" while clearly looking disappointed.

This is one reason human communication gets confusing.

People do not always say exactly what they feel. Sometimes they cannot explain their emotions clearly yet. Sometimes they are embarrassed. Sometimes they do not want attention. Sometimes they are trying to protect themselves from feeling judged, rejected, or misunderstood. And sometimes people say "I'm fine" because saying the real thing feels harder.

☆ Adults do this too.

A parent may say, "Everything's okay," while obviously feeling stressed.

A teacher may calmly say, "We'll talk later," while their expression says they are already frustrated.

Friends may pretend nothing is wrong even when tension is building underneath the conversation.

That is why listening only to words can sometimes give you the wrong picture.

People communicate with:

 words

 tone

 expressions

 energy

timing

 body language

And when those things do not match, your brain notices. Even quietly.

That strange feeling of: "They said they're okay... but something feels off."

usually comes from noticing emotional signals that do not match the words.

Signals to Notice

Sometimes a person says they are "fine" while also showing signals like:

- avoiding eye contact

- answering too quickly
- forcing a smile

- crossing their arms tightly

- speaking with a cold or shaky voice

- suddenly becoming very quiet

- looking tense or distracted

One signal alone does not prove anything. But when several signals appear together, they often reveal hidden emotions.

Real-Life Example

After soccer practice, Noah kicked his backpack onto the ground harder than usual.

"You good?" his friend Marcus asked.

"Yeah. I'm fine."

But Noah answered immediately without looking up. His face looked tight, and he kept scraping dirt with the side of his shoe.

A few seconds later, Marcus noticed Noah had barely spoken during the entire walk home.

Finally he asked, "Did something happen with Coach?"

Noah shrugged.

"He said I wasn't focused today."

There it was.
Noah had not really been fine at all.
He just was not ready to talk about it yet.

This happens constantly between friends, classmates, parents, teachers, teammates, and even adults at work. Very often, emotions leak out before people decide whether they actually want to talk about them.

That does not mean you should accuse people of lying every time their face looks different from their words.

Human emotions are messy. Some people smile when they feel nervous. Others go quiet when they feel hurt. Some become sarcastic when they feel embarrassed.

The important thing is learning to notice when the full message does not match the sentence alone.

Because socially aware people listen to more than words. They pay attention to the whole person. And once you begin noticing these hidden mismatches, conversations suddenly become easier to understand. You stop feeling confused by strange reactions. You start realizing there are emotional signals underneath almost every interaction.

Sometimes the real message is not hidden in what somebody says.

It is hidden in how they say it.

Try This

Today, listen carefully when people say simple phrases like:

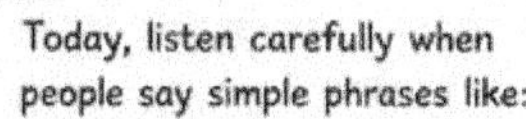

- "I'm fine."
- "Sure."
- "Whatever."
- "It's okay."
- "I don't care."

Pay attention to:

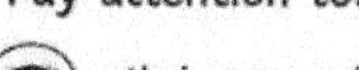

- their expression

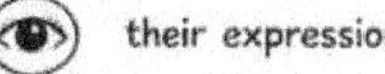

- their voice

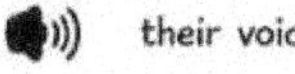

- how fast they answer

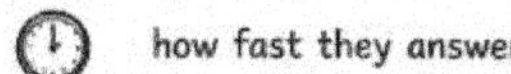

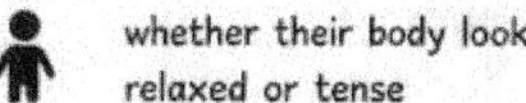

- whether their body looks relaxed or tense

You may notice something surprising.

The exact same words can mean completely different things depending on the signals around them.

That is one of the hidden rules of communication most people never explain.

The Voice Behind the Words

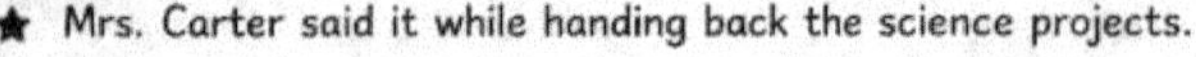

- Mrs. Carter said it while handing back the science projects.
- But something about her voice made the entire class go quiet for a second.
- The words sounded positive.
- Her tone did not.
- A few kids immediately looked at each other.
- One boy whispered, "Uh-oh."
- Nobody needed an explanation.
- They had already understood the real message.

That is the strange power of tone of voice.

People do not communicate using words alone. The way somebody says something often changes the meaning completely. A calm voice can make people feel safe. A sharp voice can make even simple words sound aggressive. A nervous voice can reveal fear before a person admits they are scared.

Sometimes the voice tells the truth faster than the words do.

That is why texting can create so many misunderstandings.
You only see the sentence — not the tone behind it.
A message like "Fine." can sound angry, annoyed, sad, sarcastic, or completely normal depending on how a person would have said it out loud.

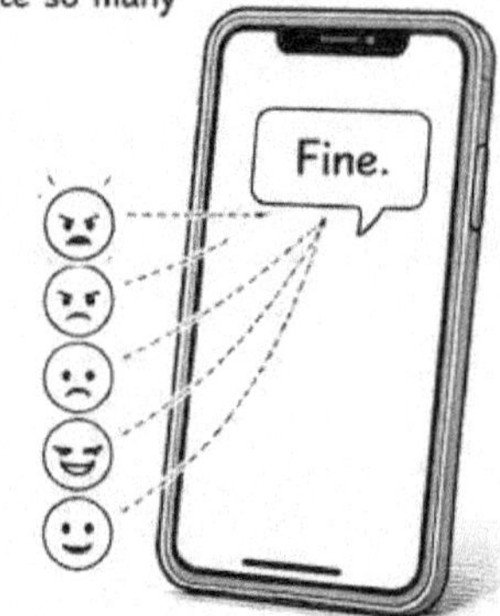

Human beings naturally listen for emotional clues inside voices.

- Volume.
- Speed.
- Energy.
- Pauses.
- Sharpness.
- Warmth.

Your brain notices all of it automatically.

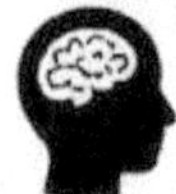

That is why someone can say, "Come here," and it can either feel comforting... or terrifying.

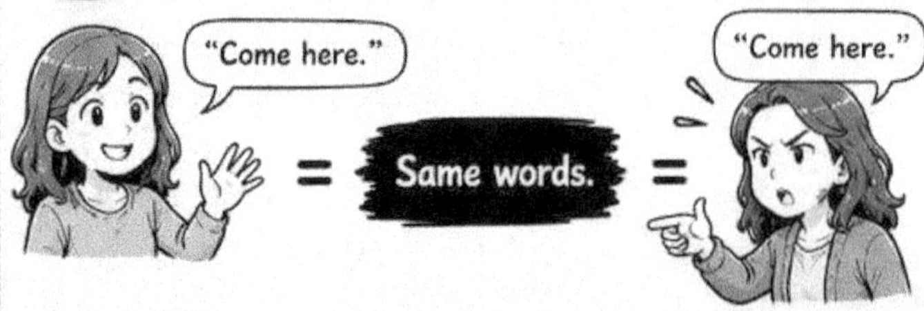

Different tone.

Completely different feeling.

Signals to Notice

Here are a few vocal signals people notice all the time:

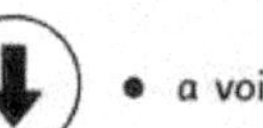

- a voice suddenly becoming quieter

- talking too fast when nervous

- forced excitement that sounds unnatural

- sharp or clipped answers

- long pauses before speaking

- sighing before answering

- a voice sounding flat or emotionless

Sometimes people try to hide emotions with words, but their voice leaks the feeling anyway.

Real-Life Example

Jordan was showing his drawing to a group of kids during art class. "Pretty cool, right?" he asked.

"Yeah. It's cool," another boy answered.

But the reply sounded stretched out and flat, almost like he was bored.

Jordan immediately lowered the paper a little.

The words themselves were not rude. But the tone made the compliment feel fake.

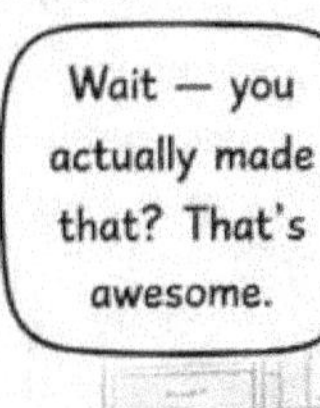

A few minutes later, another student looked at the same drawing and said, "Wait — you actually made that? That's awesome."

The sentence was simple.

But this time the excitement sounded real.

Jordan smiled instantly.

That is how powerful tone can be. Very often, people react more strongly to how something sounds than to the actual sentence itself. A warm voice can make ordinary words feel important. A cold tone can make harmless words feel insulting.

This is also why arguments sometimes explode so fast.

One person focuses on the words being said. The other reacts to the tone underneath them.

Adults say this to each other constantly. Because tone carries emotion. And emotions change everything.

Once you begin noticing tone more carefully, conversations start making a lot more sense.

You begin hearing nervousness hidden under confidence.

You notice fake excitement.

You notice when somebody sounds uncomfortable even while pretending to joke around.

You also start noticing your own voice.

- Sometimes people sound angry when they are actually stressed.
- Sometimes they sound rude without meaning to.
- Sometimes nervousness makes their voice sharper, louder, quieter, or faster than normal.

Most people are sending emotional signals through their voice all day long without even realizing it.

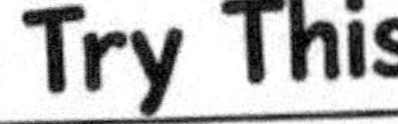

Try This

Today, pay attention to how people say simple phrases like:

- "Okay."
- "Sure."
- "Good luck."
- "Nice job."
- "Whatever."

Listen for:

 speed

 volume

 warmth

 tension

 pauses

 excitement

 irritation

You will probably notice something surprising.

The voice behind the words often changes the entire meaning.

And once you hear it, it becomes hard to ignore.

What a Smile Can Really Mean

Kayla smiled at her cousin the entire time during dinner. But something about the smile looked strange.
It appeared quickly.
Stayed too long.
And disappeared the second somebody else started talking.

Later that night, Kayla's mom quietly asked, "Did something happen between you two earlier?"

Nobody had argued at the table. Nobody had raised their voice. But sometimes smiles say more than people realize.

Most kids grow up thinking a smile always means happiness. Real life is not that simple.

Your brain notices tiny differences automatically.

A real smile usually changes the entire face. The eyes soften. The cheeks lift naturally. The expression appears relaxed instead of forced.

Fake smiles often look different.

Sometimes the mouth smiles while the eyes stay empty.

Sometimes the smile appears too fast or disappears too suddenly.

Sometimes a person smiles while the rest of their body looks tense.

People smile for many different reasons. Sometimes they smile because they are genuinely excited. Sometimes because they feel awkward. Some people smile when they are nervous. Others smile to be polite even when they are annoyed, uncomfortable, embarrassed, or trying to hide hurt feelings.

genuinely excited

feeling awkward

nervous

trying to be polite

annoyed, uncomfortable, embarrassed, or trying to hide hurt feelings

That is why some smiles instantly feel warm and real... while others feel strange almost immediately.

That does not mean every fake-looking smile is dishonest or evil. Human beings use social smiles constantly. People smile to avoid awkwardness. To stay polite. To hide nervousness. To make situations less uncomfortable.

A cashier smiles while exhausted.

A teacher smiles while stressed.

A parent smiles even during a frustrating day.

Smiles can communicate friendliness, nervousness, embarrassment, confidence, politeness, sarcasm, discomfort, or even fear depending on the situation around them.

That is why context matters.
A smile alone never tells the full story.

Signals to Notice

Here are a few differences people often notice between real and forced smiles:

- real smiles usually reach the eyes

- fake smiles often disappear quickly

- nervous smiles may appear at awkward moments

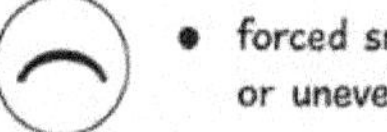

- forced smiles can look tight or uneven

- sarcastic smiles often happen on only one side of the mouth

- uncomfortable smiles may appear while someone avoids eye contact

Again, one signal alone does not prove anything.
The important thing is learning to notice patterns.

Real-Life Example

During class presentations, Ben stood at the front of the room trying to explain his project about tornadoes.

Halfway through, he accidentally skipped an entire section on his poster.

A few kids laughed quietly.

Ben smiled immediately.

But it did not look like a relaxed smile.

His shoulders tightened, and he started talking much faster than before.

The smile was not showing confidence.

It was covering embarrassment.

After class, his friend Ava walked beside him and said,

> Honestly, your project was still really good.

This time Ben smiled differently.

His face relaxed.

His eyes softened.

The second smile looked real.

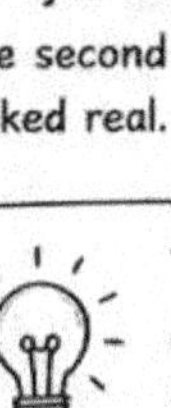

That is the difference people often feel without consciously understanding it. Some smiles create warmth and connection. Others feel tense, nervous, forced, fake, awkward, or defensive.

And human beings react to those differences constantly.

This is one reason certain people feel trustworthy very quickly. Their expressions match their emotions naturally. Nothing feels forced or overly controlled.

Other people may smile constantly but somehow still make others uncomfortable because the emotion underneath the smile feels hidden.

Expressions that match emotions feel natural and trustworthy.	Smiles that feel forced can make others uneasy.	Natural smiles create warmth and connection with others.	Hidden emotions underneath a smile can cause uncomfortableness.

Once you start noticing this, movies become more interesting too.

A character may smile while secretly feeling angry.	Another may grin while feeling insecure.	Sometimes the audience understands the truth before the other characters do.

Real life works the same way.

Smiles are not just expressions.

They are signals.

And sometimes the most important part of a smile is the emotion hiding underneath it.

Try This

Today, pay attention to different types of smiles people make.

Notice:

-  which smiles look relaxed
-  which smiles disappear quickly
-  when people smile because they feel awkward
-  when someone smiles while clearly feeling nervous
- how eyes change during genuine excitement

You will probably begin noticing something surprising.

And once you see the difference, fake smiles become much easier to spot.

The Hidden Messages in Body Language

Tyler had not said a single rude thing all afternoon. But somehow everybody at the table knew he was angry.

He dropped into his chair harder than usual. Crossed his arms tightly across his chest. Leaned away whenever somebody tried talking to him. When his friend asked if he was okay, Tyler shrugged without looking up.

"I'm good."

Nobody believed him.

That is because people communicate with their bodies constantly — even when they are completely silent.

The way someone stands, moves, sits, looks around, or reacts physically often reveals emotions faster than words do.

A confident person may walk into a room differently from someone who feels nervous. A bored student may slowly sink lower into their chair during class. Someone who feels uncomfortable may angle their body toward the exit without realizing it.

Most of this happens automatically.

Human beings are emotional creatures first and logical creatures second.

Before people carefully choose words, their body often reacts naturally to stress, excitement, fear, confidence, awkwardness, or discomfort.

That is why body language can completely change the feeling of a conversation.

A person leaning forward while listening usually feels different from someone staring at their phone.
A relaxed posture feels different from crossed arms and tight shoulders.
Someone constantly checking the room may look nervous even while pretending to act calm.

And your brain notices these signals extremely fast.
Usually before you consciously think about them.

That strange feeling of:

- "They seem uncomfortable."
- "She looks annoyed."
- "He feels confident."

often comes from body language clues happening quietly in the background.

Signals to Notice

Here are a few body language signals people notice all the time:

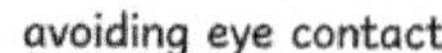
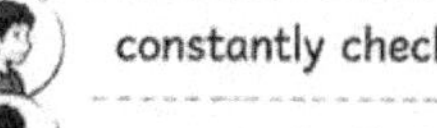
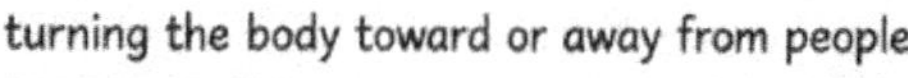
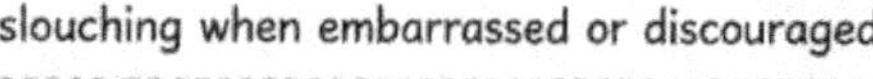

- crossed arms during tense moments
- leaning away from someone
- shoulders tightening under stress
- nervous fidgeting
- avoiding eye contact
- constantly checking the room
- turning the body toward or away from people
- slouching when embarrassed or discouraged
- standing taller when confident or excited

Again, no single movement explains everything.
But patterns tell stories.

Real-Life Example

During a group project, Sofia tried explaining her idea for the presentation.

The words sounded neutral.
His body language did not.

Even before the discussion continued, Sofia could already tell which classmate liked the idea and which one clearly did not.

This happens constantly in everyday life. People often reveal emotions physically before they admit them out loud.

A student waiting outside the principal's office may bounce their leg nonstop.

Someone embarrassed may suddenly look busy fixing their backpack.

A nervous speaker may keep adjusting their sleeves or touching their face during a presentation.

 Adults do this too.

 People at work do it.

 Teachers do it.

 Parents do it.

 Everybody does it.

Most body language is not planned.
It leaks out naturally because emotions affect the body automatically.

 Fear creates tension.

 Confidence changes posture.

 Discomfort changes movement.

 Stress changes energy.

That does not mean body language should be treated like a magic codebook where every crossed arm means anger or every lack of eye contact means lying.

- Real people are more complicated than that.
- Some people cross their arms because they are cold.
- Some avoid eye contact because they are shy or overwhelmed.
- Context always matters.

The important thing is learning to observe the whole picture instead of only listening to words.

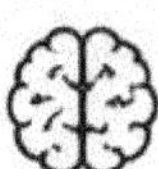

Socially aware people do this naturally.
They notice who looks comfortable together.
They notice tension before arguments start.
They notice confidence, nervousness, awkwardness, boredom, and excitement long before someone explains it directly.

And once you start noticing body language, it becomes almost impossible to stop seeing it.
You realize people are constantly speaking silently.

Try This

Today, quietly observe people's body language during conversations.

Notice:

 who leans forward while listening

 who pulls away

 who looks relaxed

 who looks tense

 how posture changes during nervous moments

how people move when they feel confident versus uncomfortable

You will probably notice something surprising.
Very often, the body tells the truth before the words do.

When Words, Voice, and Feelings Don't Match

Dad said it while gripping the steering wheel so tightly his knuckles turned white.

His jaw looked tense. His voice sounded sharp. He stared straight ahead at the road instead of looking at anyone in the car.

Technically, the words sounded calm. Everything else did not.

That uncomfortable feeling people get in moments like this usually comes from a mismatch. The words say one thing, but the voice, face, or body says something completely different.

And human brains notice those contradictions immediately.

That is one of the hidden rules of communication most people never explain.

People trust messages more when everything matches together:

- ★ the words
- ★ the tone
- ★ the facial expression
- ★ the body language
- ★ the emotion underneath it

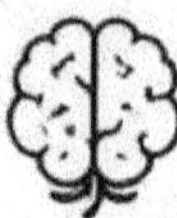

When those signals line up, communication feels natural. Clear. Easy to understand.

But when they clash, conversations suddenly feel strange.

A person may say, "I'm excited," while sounding bored.

Someone may smile while obviously feeling upset.

Another person may say, "It's fine," with a voice that sounds angry enough to start a fight.

Even little kids notice these contradictions instinctively. Because emotionally, the mixed signals feel confusing.

Signals to Notice

Here are a few common mismatches people notice all the time:

- smiling while sounding irritated
- saying "I'm fine" with a shaky voice
- calm words spoken aggressively
- fake excitement that sounds forced
- laughing while clearly uncomfortable
- relaxed words with tense body language
- polite sentences delivered coldly

Usually, when signals do not match, people trust the emotional signals more than the actual words.

Real-Life Example

During recess, Olivia accidentally bumped into another girl near the basketball court.

But the reply sounded hard and clipped.
Her smile lasted less than a second before disappearing completely. She grabbed the ball aggressively and walked away without looking back.

Olivia stood there confused for a moment.
The words had sounded forgiving.
But everything else had sounded angry.

That happens constantly in real life. Sometimes people try to hide emotions while their voice and body reveal them anyway. Other times people say polite things because they do not want conflict, even while secretly feeling frustrated, embarrassed, nervous, or hurt.

Adults do this constantly too.

A teacher may say, "Take your time," while sounding impatient.

A friend may claim they are "totally okay" while avoiding everyone for the rest of the day.

Someone may laugh during an awkward conversation while their body language screams discomfort.

This is why communication becomes confusing sometimes. People often believe they should only listen to the words being said. But socially aware people pay attention to the full message instead.

Because words alone rarely tell the entire story.

Imagine somebody saying:

"Sure. Sit with us."

Now imagine it in two different ways.

One person smiles naturally, moves their backpack, and sounds welcoming.

Another keeps their arms crossed, avoids eye contact, and says it with a flat voice while nobody makes room at the table.

Same sentence.
Completely different emotional message.

That is because emotions leak through behavior constantly. Human beings are not robots carefully controlling every expression, movement, and tone perfectly. Feelings slip out through tiny signals all the time.

And once you notice this, the social world starts becoming easier to read.

- You begin understanding why certain conversations feel fake.
- Why some people make others uncomfortable without openly saying anything rude.
- Why tension can exist even when everybody is technically "being nice."

You also begin noticing your own mixed signals.

- Sometimes you may think you sound calm while actually sounding defensive.
- Sometimes you may smile while clearly looking uncomfortable.
- Sometimes your words say one thing while your emotions quietly reveal another.

Everybody sends mixed signals sometimes.
The important thing is learning to notice them instead of ignoring them.

Because very often, the truth hides in the mismatch.

Try This

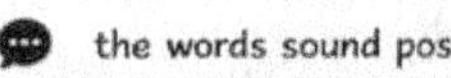
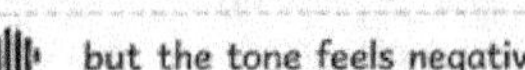

Today, pay attention to moments when:

 the words sound positive

 but the tone feels negative

or the expression looks uncomfortable

or the body language feels tense

Notice:

- which signal feels more believable
- how people react to mixed emotions
- how awkward conversations often contain mismatched signals

You will probably discover something surprising.
People do not only listen to words.
They listen to whether everything matches together.

PART II

THE SIGNALS YOU SEND WITHOUT KNOWING

Most people think they are only communicating when they choose to.

But your brain is sending signals all the time.
Even when you say nothing.
Even when you are trying to hide how you feel.

Your face changes when you feel nervous.

Your posture changes when you feel confident.

Your voice changes when you feel uncomfortable.

Your energy changes when you walk into a room upset, excited, embarrassed, or stressed.

And other people notice more of those signals than you realize.
Not because they are analyzing you.
Because human brains are constantly reading emotional information automatically.

That means people often react to signals you never meant to send.

- ★ A crossed-arm posture can make you seem closed off.
- ★ Looking at the floor too much can make you seem unsure of yourself.
- ★ Speaking too fast can make people feel your nervousness.
- ★ A calm voice can make people trust you more instantly.

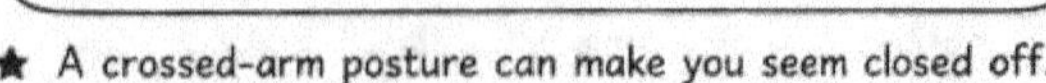

Sometimes people respond more to your emotional signals... than to your actual words.

That is why two people can say the exact same sentence — and create completely different reactions.

One person walks into a room and everyone relaxes.

Another walks in and the whole mood changes immediately.

Not because of magic. Signals.

Tiny emotional clues people feel before they consciously explain them.

This section is about becoming aware of the signals you send without realizing it.

Not so you become fake.
Not so you overthink every movement.
And definitely not so you try to "perform" all the time.

Real confidence usually feels natural.
But awareness changes things.

Because once you notice your own habits... you start understanding why certain social moments happen the way they do.

You notice:

- ★ when your nervousness shows physically
- ★ when your body becomes defensive
- ★ when your energy affects a group
- ★ when people mirror each other automatically
- ★ when confidence looks calm instead of loud

One of the strangest parts of being human is this: other people often feel your emotional state before you explain it.

That is why someone can walk into class looking upset...

and everybody suddenly acts quieter.

Or why one relaxed person can calm down an entire group.

Humans affect each other constantly.
Usually without realizing it.

And once you start noticing those invisible signals... you begin understanding why some people naturally draw others in — while others accidentally push people away without meaning to.

The good news?

Social awareness is not something you are simply "born with."
A lot of it comes from noticing patterns.
And the more clearly you notice those patterns...
the easiey people start making sense.

The Face You Make When You Feel Nervous

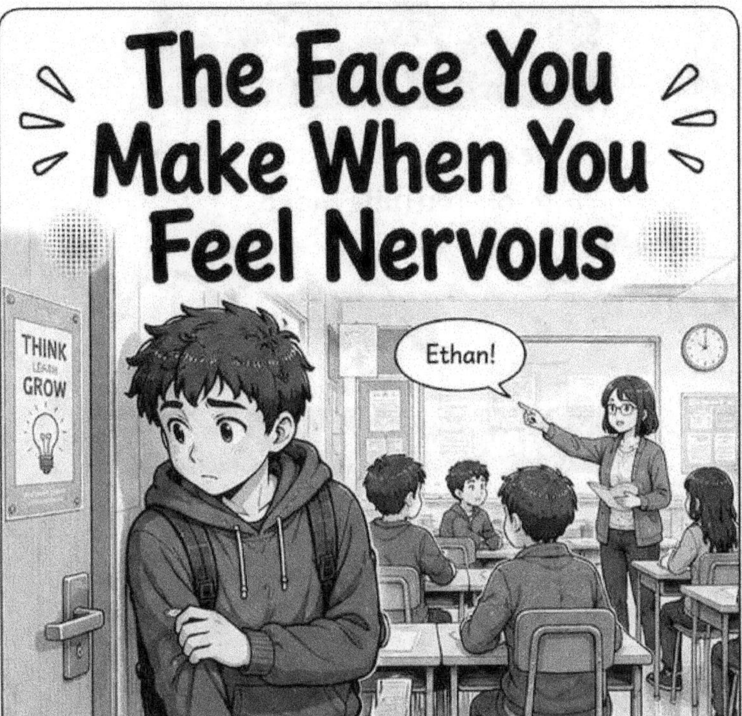

Ethan stood near the classroom door pretending to look at a poster on the wall. But he wasn't really reading it.

★ His shoulders looked tight.
★ His smile appeared for one second… then disappeared.
★ He kept touching the sleeve of his hoodie.

Mrs. Carter called his name.
Ethan answered too quickly.

"Yeah. Yep. I'm here."

The class barely noticed.
But Maya did.

Something about his face looked… uncomfortable.

Not sad.
Not angry.
Just nervous.

People often think nervousness only happens inside the brain. But the body usually shows it first.

A fast smile.

Tight lips.

Looking away too quickly.

Blinking more than normal.

Touching your face.

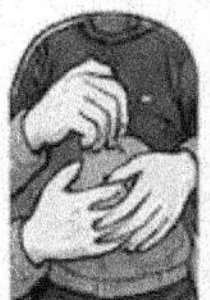
Fidgeting with your hands.

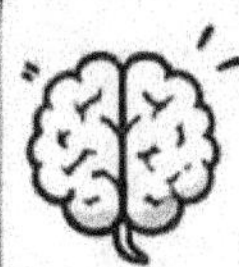

Sometimes a person's face looks calm… but tiny signals start leaking out anyway. Your brain notices these signals even when you don't realize it.

That's one reason people sometimes say:

"You seem nervous."

Even when nobody said a word.

Signals to Notice

 Smiles that disappear very fast

 Tight jaw or pressed lips

 Looking away suddenly

 Touching hair, sleeves, or face repeatedly

 Fast blinking

 Forced laughing

 Eyebrows pulling together for a second

None of these signals guarantee someone feels nervous.

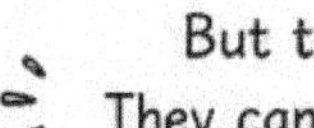

But together?
They can tell a story.

Real-Life Example

A girl stands in front of the class holding her presentation notes.

But her voice sounds thinner than usual.

She keeps shifting her weight.

Her fingers squeeze the paper tightly.

The class hears the words.

But their brains also notice the signals.

That's the hidden part of communication most people never explain.

 Try This

The next time you watch a movie or YouTube video,

mute the sound for thirty seconds.

Just watch people's faces.

Can you tell:

- who feels nervous?

- who feels confident?

- who feels uncomfortable pretending to be calm?

You'll start noticing signals everywhere.

And once you see them... it becomes hard to unsee them.

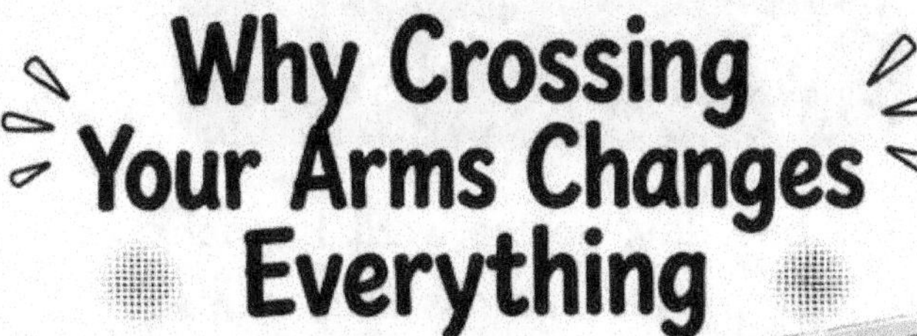

Why Crossing Your Arms Changes Everything

Noah walked into the group late. Three kids were already talking near the window.

But his arms stayed crossed tightly across his chest.

Noah stopped for half a second. Something suddenly felt... closed.

Not exactly rude.
Not exactly angry.
Just hard to enter.

That's the strange thing about body language. Sometimes the body speaks louder than the face. Crossing your arms is one of the biggest examples.

People cross their arms for many reasons.

Sometimes they're cold.

Sometimes they feel awkward.

Sometimes they're protecting themselves without realizing it.

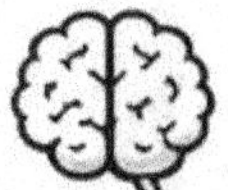

But other people's brains often read the signal as:

- closed off
- uncomfortable
- defensive
- annoyed
- uninterested

Even when none of that is true.

This is why body language changes the mood of a conversation so fast.

The signal reaches people before the explanation does.

A person may mean:

"I feel nervous."

But their body accidentally says:

"Stay back."

Signals to Notice

Arms pulled tightly against the chest

Hands hidden

Shoulders raised slightly

Leaning away from people

Elbows locked close to the body

Little movement while talking

One signal alone doesn't explain everything.

But patterns matter.
Especially in groups.

Real-Life Example

A teacher asks a question during class discussion.

One student answers while sitting with open posture, relaxed shoulders, and moving hands.

Another student gives almost the exact same answer...
but keeps their arms crossed tightly and avoids eye contact.

The class reacts differently to each person.

Not because of the words.

Because of the feeling their body language creates.

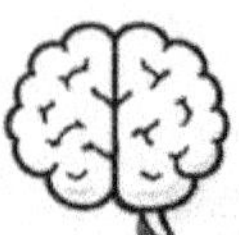

Most people don't even realize they're doing this.
Their brains just respond automatically.

Try This

For one day, notice what happens when people uncross their arms during conversations.

Watch the room carefully.

Does the energy change?

Do people seem easier to approach?

Then try it yourself.

The next time you feel nervous, let your arms relax at your sides for a moment.

You might still feel nervous inside...

but the signal you send to other people completely changes.

And sometimes...
that changes
the entire conversation.

Looking Confident Even When You Feel Scared

Ava could feel her heart pounding before she even stood up.

Her hands felt cold.

Her stomach twisted.

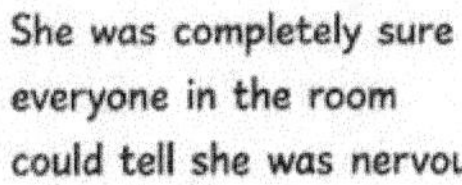

She was completely sure everyone in the room could tell she was nervous.

Then she looked at the girl presenting before her.

- ✔ The girl sounded calm.
- ✔ Confident.
- ✔ Totally relaxed.

But when Ava looked closer...

...she noticed the girl was holding her note cards so tightly the edges were bent.

That's something most people never realize.
Confident people are not always fearless people.
Sometimes they're nervous too.
They've just learned how to <u>control</u> the signals they send.

Because confidence is not only a feeling.
It's also a message.

People often decide whether someone seems confident within seconds.
Before the person even finishes speaking.

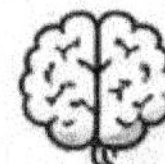

That's one of the hidden rules of social life:
People react to what they <u>see</u>...
not just what you <u>feel</u>.

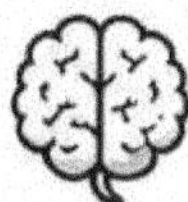

The brain notices:

- posture
- eye contact
- movement
- voice pace
- facial tension
- energy

A shaky <u>voice</u> can make someone seem uncertain.

A calm pause can make someone seem strong.

Even when both <u>people</u> feel equally scared <u>inside</u>.

Signals to Notice

People who <u>look</u> confident often:

 move more slowly

 keep their shoulders relaxed

 make eye contact for a moment longer

 pause before answering

 keep their face calmer

 avoid rushing their words

 take up space naturally instead of shrinking

None of this means they never feel nervous.
Usually it means they've <u>practiced</u> <u>staying</u> <u>calm</u> <u>while</u> <u>nervous</u>.

That's different.

Real-Life Example

Two students walk into the same classroom late.

The first rushes in fast.

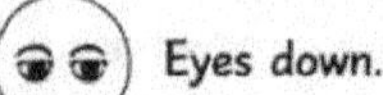 Eyes down.

 Backpack slipping off one shoulder.

 Voice tense.

The second student is probably nervous too.

 But they slow down first.

 Shoulders relaxed.

 Head up.

 Voice calm.

 Same situation.
Completely different energy. 

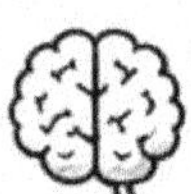 **The room reacts differently immediately.** 

 Not because one student is "better."

 Because people respond to signals before explanations.

 Try This

The next time you feel nervous before talking to someone, try changing <u>only one</u> signal.

 **Not everything.**
Just one. 

Maybe:

 slow down your walking

 relax your shoulders

 pause before answering

 breathe once before speaking

 keep your head up for two extra seconds

 **Small changes matter more than people think.** 

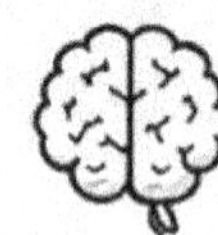 Sometimes confidence does not start with feeling brave.

Sometimes it starts with looking calm long enough for your brain to catch up. 

The Difference Between Calm and Weak

The room got louder after the argument started.
Two kids were talking over each other.
Chairs scraped the floor.
Someone muttered, "Here we go again."

But Jordan stayed quiet.
He didn't yell.
Didn't interrupt.
Didn't roll his eyes.
He just listened for a second before speaking.

And somehow...
the room started calming down around him.

A lot of people confuse calmness with weakness.
But they are not the same thing at all.

Weakness often looks like:

 avoiding everything

 backing down from fear

 saying nothing because you feel powerless

 shrinking yourself to disappear

Real calmness feels different.

Calm people usually:

 stay steady under pressure

 speak without rushing

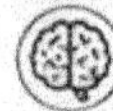 control their reactions

 think before exploding

 make other people feel less chaotic

That's why the calmest person in the room sometimes becomes the most powerful one.

 Not because they are loud.

 Because they make everyone else feel more stable.

 People trust calm energy.

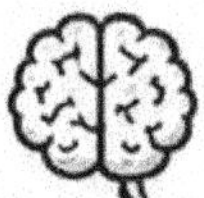

Especially during stressful moments.
Your brain automatically notices who seems emotionally "safe."
And most of the time...
it's not the loudest person.

Signals to Notice

Calm people often:

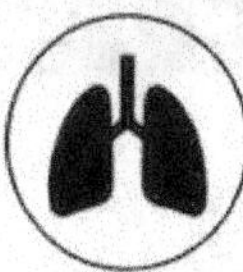 breathe more slowly

 pause before reacting

 keep their movements controlled

 use steady voices

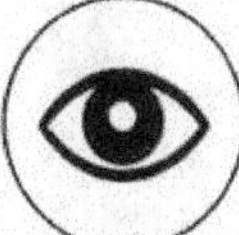 hold eye contact without staring

 avoid dramatic reactions

 stay grounded when others become emotional

This does not mean they never feel upset.

It means they don't let every feeling take control of the room.

Real-Life Example

Try This

During a group project,
two students disagree.

One student immediately gets louder.

The other student stays calm.

Nobody says it out loud... but the group starts paying attention to the calmer person.

Because calmness often feels stronger than emotional chaos.

Even adults forget this sometimes.

The next time something awkward or annoying happens, wait <u>two extra seconds</u> before reacting.

Not forever.
Just <u>two</u> seconds.

Notice what changes.

Sometimes the strongest social skill is not reacting instantly.

Sometimes real confidence looks surprisingly <u>quiet</u>.

The Energy You Bring Into a Room

Before Liam even sat down, the group project already felt different.
Nobody could fully explain why.
He hadn't said anything important yet.
He hadn't made jokes.
He hadn't acted loud or dramatic.
But somehow...
the room felt lighter when he walked in.

That's something people notice more than they realize:
Every person brings a certain energy into a room.

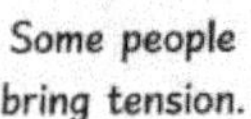

Some people bring tension.

Some bring calm.

Some bring chaos.

Some make everybody quieter.

Some make people relax immediately.

And most of this happens without words.

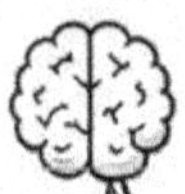

Your brain is constantly asking invisible questions like:

- Does this person feel safe?
- Do they seem angry?
- Nervous?
- Confident?
- Judging everyone?
- Happy to be here?

The answers usually come from signals.
Not speeches.

A person who storms into a room fast, drops their bag loudly, and sighs heavily changes the mood instantly.

A person who enters calmly, notices people, and feels emotionally steady changes the mood too.

Energy spreads faster than people think.
That's why one anxious person can make a whole group nervous. And one calm person can make everyone breathe easier.

Signals to Notice

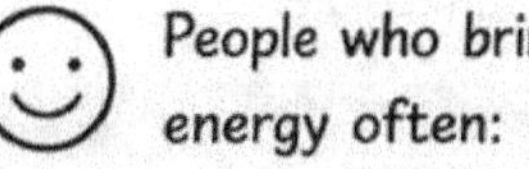

People who bring calm, positive energy often:

move without rushing

make people feel noticed

smile naturally instead of forcing it

keep their voices steady

react without overreacting

listen without looking bored

make the room feel emotionally safer

Meanwhile, tense energy often looks like:

heavy sighing

irritated tone

restless movements

negative reactions to everything

making others feel judged or uncomfortable

Most people feel these signals immediately.
Even if they cannot explain them.

Real-Life Example

Two students join the same lunch table.

The first drops into the chair and immediately complains.

Nobody answers much after that.

The second student sits down smiling slightly.

The conversation opens back up again almost instantly.

Same table.
Different energy.
Different reaction.

 Try This

Tomorrow, pay attention to how different people make a room feel.

Not what they say first.

What they bring first.

Then notice your own energy too.

Do people seem more relaxed after talking to you?

More tense?

More open?

You don't have to become the loudest person in the room to change its energy.

Sometimes the people who affect a room the most...

barely speak at all.

Why People Copy Each Other Without Realizing

At the beginning of lunch, everyone at the table sounded tired.
Nobody was talking much.
People kept looking at their phones.
The energy felt flat.

Then Sofia started laughing at something.
A real laugh.

A few seconds later, two other people smiled too.

Suddenly the whole table felt different.
More awake. More relaxed. More connected.
Nobody planned it.
It just happened.

People affect each other more than they realize.

Groups especially do this all the time.
That's why school hallways, classrooms, and lunch tables can suddenly change mood so quickly.

Humans copy each other constantly without realizing it.

Not only words.
Also:

- facial expressions
- posture
- tone of voice
- energy
- laughing
- yawning
- emotional reactions

This happens because the brain is always observing other people.
And sometimes...
it quietly starts matching them.

That's one reason moods spread through groups so fast.

One nervous person can make everyone tense.

One calm person can settle the room down.

One excited person can suddenly make everybody louder.

Scientists sometimes call this mirroring.
But most people never notice they're doing it.

Signals to Notice

People often copy:

- smiles
- crossed arms
- leaning forward
- whispering
- excitement
- nervous laughter
- phone-checking
- even the speed of walking

Real-Life Example

A student walks into class stressed and frustrated.

He drops his backpack hard onto the floor.

"Great. Another test."

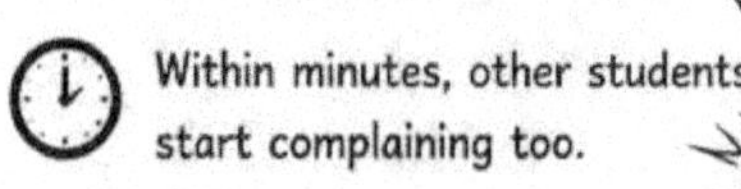

Within minutes, other students start complaining too.

The energy spreads across the room.

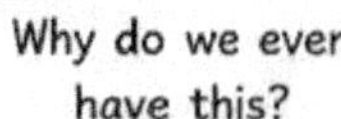

But later, another student says:

Now the mood shifts again.

Same classroom.
Different emotional signal.
Different result.

One small signal can change everyone's experience.
That's the power of human mirroring.

Try This

Tomorrow, watch what happens when one person starts laughing in a group.

Or when one person becomes nervous.

Notice how quickly other people start matching the energy.

Then try a small experiment yourself.
During a conversation:

- speak a little calmer
- slow your movements slightly

- smile naturally once

- relax your shoulders

See if the other person slowly begins copying you.
Because people are constantly sending signals to each other...
and constantly receiving them too.
Most of it happens silently.

PART III

SCHOOL IS FULL OF SIGNALS

School is not just homework, classes, and tests.
It is one giant social environment.

Every hallway.
Every lunch table.
Every group project.
Every classroom.

Filled with invisible signals people are constantly sending to each other.

- ★ Some kids walk into class and instantly become louder around friends.
- ★ Some go completely quiet when certain people are nearby.
- ★ Some teachers can calm down a room without raising their voice once.
- ★ Others lose control of the class before the lesson even starts.

And somehow... everybody feels these shifts almost immediately.

That is because schools are emotional ecosystems.
People are constantly watching:

- ★ who gets attention
- ★ who gets ignored
- ★ who seems confident
- ★ who feels awkward
- ★ who belongs where
- ★ who controls the mood of the group

Most of this happens silently.

A single look across the classroom can communicate: "Don't say that."

A group laugh can make somebody feel included... or completely embarrassed.

A teacher pausing before answering can suddenly make the whole room tense.

And sometimes the strongest social moments happen without anybody saying anything directly at all.

That is why school can feel emotionally exhausting sometimes.

Your brain is tracking hundreds of tiny social signals every day:

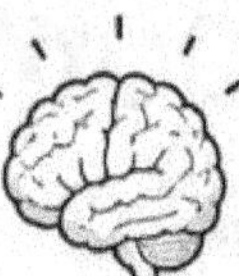

- ★ facial reactions
- ★ tone changes
- ★ eye contact
- ★ group behavior
- ★ awkward silences
- ★ shifting moods
- ★ who people sit beside
- ★ who gets interrupted
- ★ who everybody watches when something happens

Even walking into the cafeteria can feel like entering a room filled with invisible rules.

→ Where do you sit?
→ Who notices you?
→ Who pretends not to?
→ Who seems relaxed?
→ Who seems like they are trying too hard?

School teaches social awareness constantly... even when nobody explains it out loud.

And sometimes kids secretly believe:

"Everybody else understands this except me."

But the truth is:

- ★ most people are confused sometimes.
- ★ most people overthink social moments sometimes.
- ★ most people misread situations sometimes.

Because human communication is messy.
Especially in groups.
Especially during school years when everybody is still figuring themselves out.

This section is about learning to notice those hidden social patterns more clearly.
Not to become paranoid.
Not to judge everybody.
But to understand why school sometimes feels easy... and other times feels emotionally complicated for reasons nobody explains.

Because once you start noticing the signals underneath school life...
a lot of confusing moments suddenly start making more sense.

Reading the Classroom Mood

The second the teacher walked in, everybody felt it.
Something was different.
The room got quieter without anyone asking.
A few students quickly put their phones away.
Even the loud table near the back
stopped talking for a moment.
Nobody announced: **"Today feels tense."**

But somehow...
everyone already knew.

Classrooms have moods. Just like people do.

Some days the room feels relaxed.
Some days it feels **heavy.**
Some days **everybody** seems restless
at the same time.
And most of the signals are invisible
unless you start paying attention.

Humans are constantly scanning groups for emotional information.

Your brain notices:

- noise level
- movement
- facial expressions
- teacher energy
- tension between students
- excitement
- awkward silence

All of this creates what people call "the vibe."
Even if nobody says it out loud.

That's why walking into a classroom can sometimes feel easy... or instantly uncomfortable. Before anything even happens.

Signals to Notice

A classroom that feels <u>tense</u> often has:

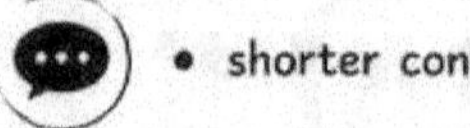
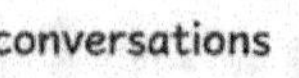

- shorter conversations

- nervous laughter

- less movement

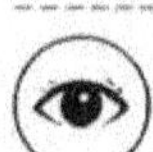

- people avoiding eye contact

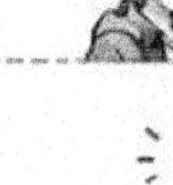

- fast reactions from the teacher

- whispering

- heavy silence after someone talks

A <u>**relaxed**</u> classroom often has:

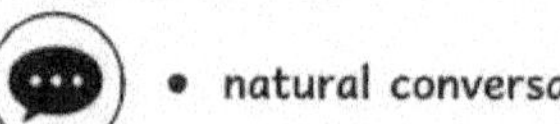

- natural conversation

- loose body language

- people joking comfortably

- calmer voices

- more movement and openness

The mood spreads fast. Especially in groups.

Real-Life Example

A teacher starts handing back test papers.
The room changes <u>immediately.</u>

★ Students sit up straighter.
★ Some people stop talking.
★ One student laughs nervously.
★ Nobody planned it.

The emotional signal simply spread through the classroom.

Now imagine a different day.
The teacher walks in smiling slightly.

"Good news.
No homework tonight."

↓

Suddenly:

- shoulders relax
- people lean forward
- conversations restart
- energy changes everywhere at once

Groups react emotionally together all the time.
Most people just never notice it happening.

Try This

Tomorrow at school, pause for five seconds before class starts.

Don't focus on one person.
Focus on the <u>whole room.</u>

Ask yourself:

- Does the room feel calm or tense?
- Loud or careful?
- Comfortable or awkward?
- Focused or distracted?

↓

Then try guessing why the mood feels that way.

The more you practice noticing group signals...
the more social situations start <u>making sense.</u>

When the Teacher Is Actually Annoyed

- ★ But the room suddenly went quiet.
- ★ A few students looked down at their desks.
- ★ One kid stopped laughing immediately.
- ★ The words sounded calm.
- ★ But something underneath them didn't.

That's because people do not only listen to what someone says. They also listen to:

- tone
- speed
- facial tension
- pauses
- eye contact
- energy

And teachers are masters of this.

Sometimes a teacher looks relaxed...
while secretly becoming more and more annoyed.
Most students can feel it before the teacher says anything directly.
The signals start leaking out first.

- → A tighter smile.
- → A slower voice.
- → Longer pauses.
- → Sharp eye contact.
- → Very controlled calmness.

That's one of the hidden rules of communication:
The calmer someone sounds...
the more carefully you should sometimes listen.
<u>**Especially adults.**</u>

People hear everything.
But they do not always realize what it means right away.

Signals to Notice

Teachers often seem annoyed when they:

- repeat instructions very slowly 
- stop smiling suddenly 
- pause before answering 
- use extra calm voices 
- stare longer than usual 
- press their lips together 
- stop joking with the class 

Sometimes the room notices these signals before the students causing the problem do.
That's why everybody suddenly gets quieter at the same time.

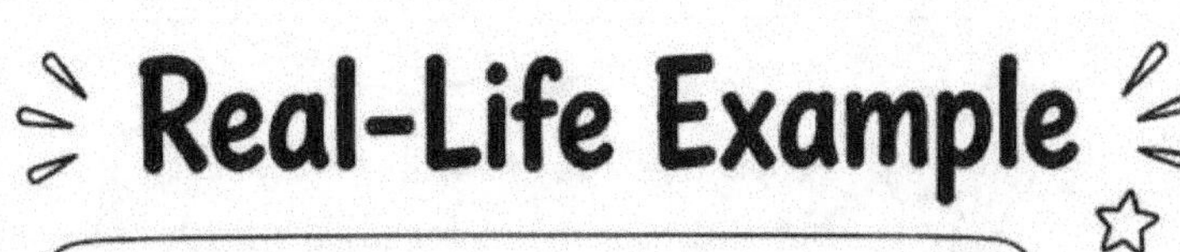

☆ Two students keep whispering during class.

☆ Finally the teacher stops talking.
The room becomes silent.

☆ Then the teacher says:

"Do you two want to teach the lesson today?"

☆ The class laughs nervously.

Not because the teacher yelled.
Because everyone heard the signal underneath the words.
The voice sounded controlled.
Too controlled.
And suddenly everybody understood:

Okay. She's actually annoyed now.

The next time an adult says:

"That's fine."

➡ Pause for a second.

➡ Ask yourself:

Did it actually sound fine?

Notice:

- facial expression

- tone

- pacing

- eye contact

Sometimes words tell one story...
while the voice tells the real one.

☆ And once you start noticing
the difference...
school starts becoming
much easier to read..

Group Projects and Silent Drama

- Eli said it while looking at his Chromebook.
- But the way he said it made the entire table feel weird.
- Nobody answered for a second.
- One student suddenly became very interested in their pencil.
- Another forced a small laugh.
- The group project had officially entered silent drama mode.

Almost every group project has two conversations happening at the same time.

The first conversation is obvious:

The second conversation is invisible:

- Who feels ignored?
- Who wants control?
- Who feels annoyed?
- Who is pretending to agree?
- Who has stopped trying?

Most of these feelings are never said directly. People signal them instead.

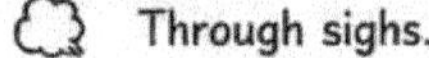

- Through sighs.
- Silence.
- Tone changes.
- Eye contact.
- Tiny facial expressions.

That's why group projects can become uncomfortable so fast even when nobody is openly fighting.

Humans are extremely good at sensing tension inside groups. Especially hidden tension.

People rarely say how they really feel. But their signals usually tell the truth before their words do.

Signals to Notice

Silent drama often looks like:

- fake agreement

- forced smiling

- heavy sighs

- people interrupting more

- one person becoming unusually quiet

- side glances between friends

- sarcastic tone

- someone saying "I don't care" too fast

One signal alone may mean nothing.

But together?

The emotional story becomes easier to see.

Real-Life Example

Four students are choosing roles for a presentation.

Nobody responds immediately.

But suddenly:

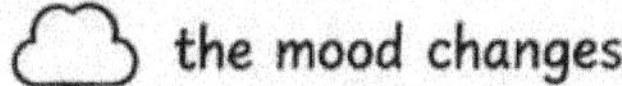

- the mood changes

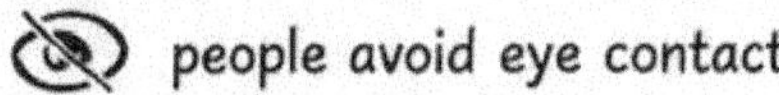

- people avoid eye contact

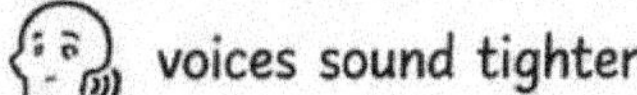

- voices sound tighter
- the conversation becomes awkward

Why?

Because the sentence wasn't only about the project.
It was also a social signal:

"I feel unappreciated."

And everybody at the table felt it instantly.
Even without discussing it directly.

Try This

During your next group activity, pay attention to the moments between the words.

Notice:

sudden silence

nervous laughter

tone shifts

people pulling away emotionally

fake *"it's fine"* energy

Ask yourself:

What is the group ***feeling*** right now?
Not just saying.

The people who understand group dynamics best are usually not the loudest people.

They're the people quietly noticing what everyone else misses.

The Invisible Rules of the Lunch Table

Mia stood at the edge of the cafeteria holding her tray.

- ★ Every table looked full somehow. Even the ones with empty seats.
- ★ One group was laughing loudly near the windows.
- ★ Another table barely looked up when she walked past.
- ★ At one table, backpacks were placed on the empty chairs like invisible signs saying: "Taken."

Nobody explains this when you start school.
Lunch tables have rules.
Invisible ones.
And almost everybody learns them silently.

Who sits where. Who talks first.
Who gets interrupted. Who gets saved a seat.
Who gets ignored.

Most of these rules are never spoken out loud.
But people feel them immediately.

That's why lunch tables can sometimes feel safe... or terrifying.

In just a few seconds, your brain starts scanning for signals:

- Do these people want me here?
- Am I interrupting something?
- Who has the most social power?
- Does this group feel open or closed?

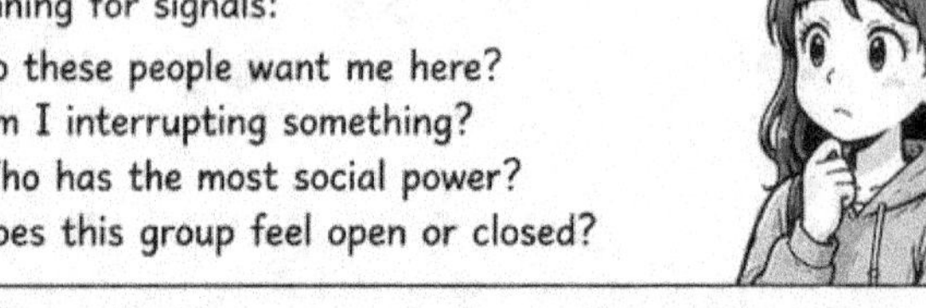

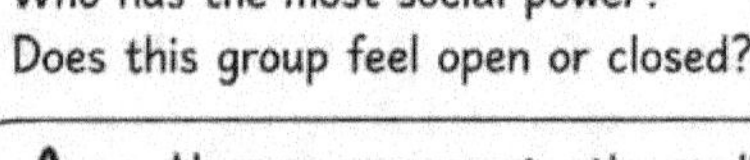

Humans are constantly reading social territory. Especially in groups.

Signals you miss... shape the experiences you have.

Signals to Notice

Our brains are always collecting clues. Here are some of the most important ones at the lunch table.

A lunch table that feels welcoming often has:

-  open body language
-  eye contact when someone approaches
-  people making space naturally
-  relaxed conversation
-  smiling that feels real

A table that feels "closed" often has:

-  backpacks blocking seats
-  people avoiding eye contact
-  inside jokes nonstop
-  tight group posture
-  quick glances at each other when someone approaches

Nobody may say:

"You can't sit here."

But the signals can still say it loudly.

Real-Life Example

A student walks toward a table and asks:

One person says:

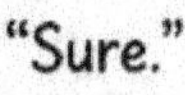

- ✕ But nobody moves their backpack.
- ✕ Nobody looks up.
- ✕ Nobody makes space.

The words say yes.
The signals say something completely different.

Now imagine another table.

The difference feels enormous.
Even before the conversation starts.

Try This

The next time you enter a cafeteria, pause before sitting down.

Look carefully at different tables.

Which ones feel:

- open?

- tense?

- welcoming?

- controlled by one person?

- awkward?

Then notice something else:

What signals does your table send to other people?

Sometimes kids feel invisible at school...
not because something is wrong with them...
but because nobody ever explained the hidden social rules everyone else was quietly learning.

Knowing When to Speak Up

- ★ The classroom stayed silent after Noah's idea. Too silent.
- ★ He could feel it immediately.
- ★ A few students looked at each other.
- ★ Someone shrugged slightly.
- ★ The teacher waited.
- ★ Noah suddenly wished he had never raised his hand at all.

Then, from the back of the room, another student said:

"Actually...
I think that idea
could work."

↓

The whole mood shifted.
Just a little.
But enough.

Sometimes speaking up changes more than people realize.
And sometimes staying silent changes things too.

One of the hardest social skills in the world is knowing when to talk.
Not talking constantly.
Not staying quiet forever.
Reading the moment.

Some people interrupt every silence because silence makes them nervous.

Other people stay quiet because they are afraid of being judged.

But socially aware people learn something important:

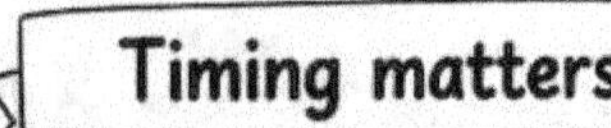

Timing matters.

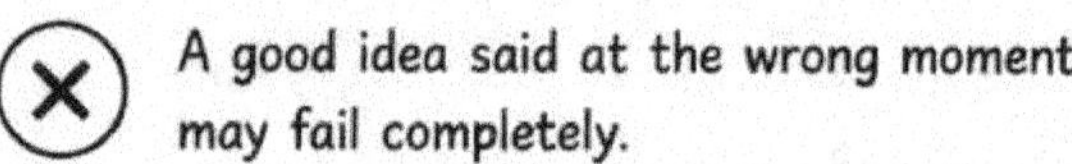

A good idea said at the wrong moment may fail completely.

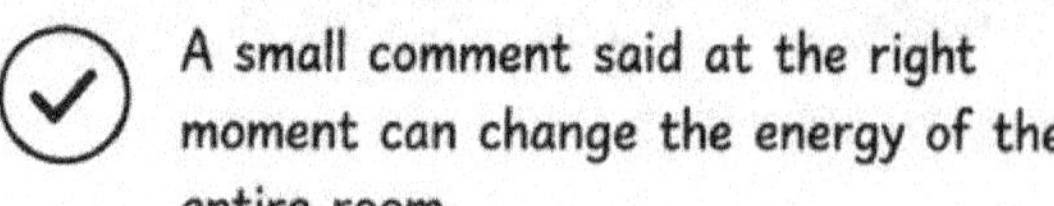

A small comment said at the right moment can change the energy of the entire room.

Signals to Notice

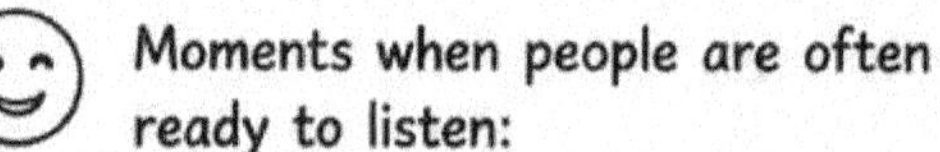

Moments when people are often ready to listen:

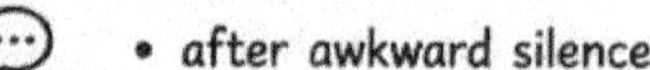

- after awkward silence
- when everybody seems confused
- when tension starts building
- when someone looks unsupported
- when the group needs direction
- when nobody else wants to speak first

Moments when people may stop listening:

- constant interrupting
- talking too long
- speaking only to get attention
- ignoring the mood of the room
- forcing jokes during serious moments

People usually remember how someone felt in a conversation more than the exact words they said.

Real-Life Example

During a group discussion, everybody keeps arguing about small details.

The conversation goes in circles. Finally one student says calmly:

"Wait. I think we're talking about two different problems."

The room pauses.

Suddenly everybody relaxes slightly.

Why?

Because the student noticed the emotional moment and the right time to speak. ♡

That's <u>real</u> communication skill.

Not being the loudest person. Helping the room move forward.

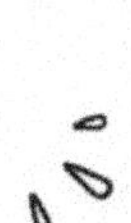

Try This

Tomorrow, pay attention to the moments right <u>before</u> someone speaks.

Notice:

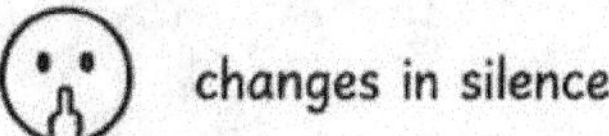

changes in silence

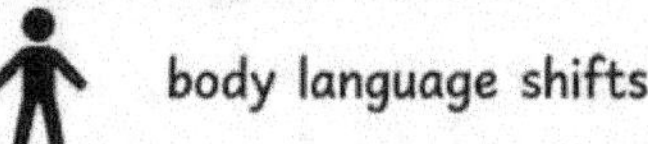

body language shifts

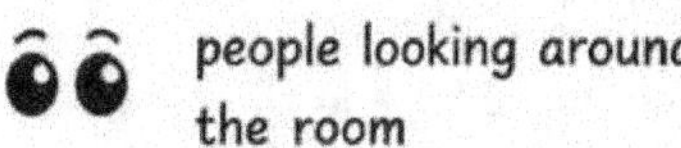

people looking around the room

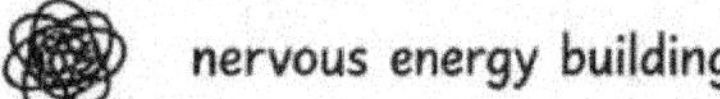

nervous energy building

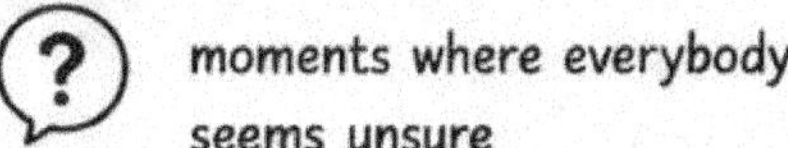

moments where everybody seems unsure

Then ask yourself:

Would speaking right now help the situation... or only add more noise?

The people who understand social situations best are often not the people talking nonstop.

They're the people paying attention to timing.

The Fastest Way to Lose a Room

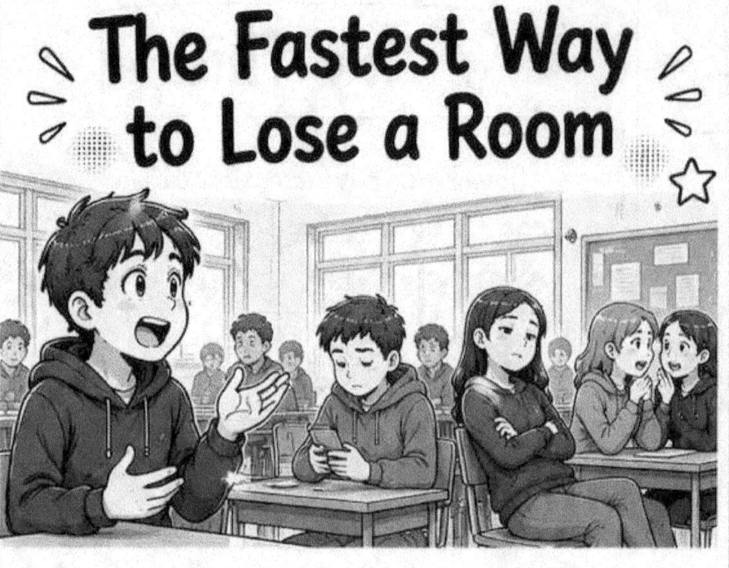

- ★ Evan kept talking long after everyone stopped listening.
- ★ At first, people nodded politely.
- ★ Then someone checked their phone.
- ★ Another student leaned back in their chair.
- ★ One girl quietly started another conversation beside him.
- ★ But Evan didn't notice. He just kept going.

A lot of people think losing a room happens suddenly.
Usually it doesn't.
It happens slowly.
Signal by signal.

Humans constantly show when their attention is disappearing.
The problem is:
many people only focus on their own words...
instead of the reactions around them.

That's one of the hidden rules of communication:
Good communicators do not only express themselves.
They read the room while talking.

Because sometimes the fastest way to lose people is:

- talking too long
- trying too hard to impress
- making everything about yourself
- ignoring other people's reactions
- forcing energy that feels fake
- continuing after the emotional moment has already passed

When people feel trapped in a conversation, their body language changes first. Long before they say anything directly.

Signals to Notice

People often start disconnecting when they:

 stop making eye contact

 look around the room

 fake small laughs

 shift their body away

 interrupt more often

 give shorter answers

 check phones or backpacks

 stop reacting emotionally

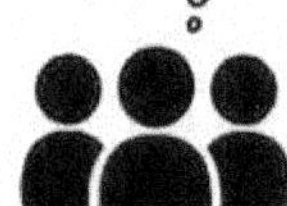

Sometimes nobody says:

"This conversation is getting awkward."

But everybody feels it.

Real-Life Example

A student starts telling a story during lunch.

At first everybody listens.
But the story keeps getting longer.
And longer.

Soon:

 people stop asking questions

 someone starts talking quietly to another friend

 another student stares at the cafeteria line

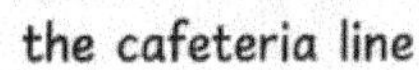

 the energy slowly dies

The storyteller keeps trying harder to make the story funny. But that usually makes it worse.

 Why?

Because people feel most comfortable in conversations where energy moves naturally.
Not where one person controls the entire room.

Try This

The next time you talk in a group, notice what happens around your words. Not just your story.

Watch for:

 eye contact

 posture shifts

 attention changes

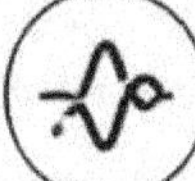 energy dropping or rising

 people leaning in... or pulling away

The best communicators are not the people who talk the most.

They are the people who notice when the room is still with them. And when it isn't anymore.

PART IV

FRIENDSHIP CAN GET CONFUSING

Friendships are built on emotional signals constantly changing underneath the surface.

Friendship seems simple from the outside.
Two people laugh together. Sit together. Text each other. Hang out at school. Easy.
Except... it usually is not.
Because friendships are filled with invisible emotions people do not always explain clearly.

TINY SIGNALS YOU MIGHT MISS

 A slower reply.

 A colder tone.

 A fake laugh.

 A missing invitation.

A strange silence after you say something.

Your brain notices these things automatically.
That is why friendships can sometimes feel emotionally confusing even when nothing "big" happened.

One strange truth about friendship is this: people often reveal how they feel through patterns... before they say it out loud.

That is why someone can claim: "Nothing's wrong."

While slowly becoming harder to reach.

Or why somebody can laugh with you...

while secretly trying to impress the group more than connect with you.

Because friendship is mostly an emotional world happening under the surface.

One day somebody acts normal. The next day they feel distant.
Someone says: "I'm joking." But the joke somehow feels mean.
A friend acts completely different around certain people.
A group laugh suddenly makes you feel excluded instead of included.

And sometimes the most confusing part is this:
nobody says anything directly wrong.
But something still feels different.

Humans are extremely sensitive to belonging.
Especially during school years.

People want to feel:

- included
- chosen
- understood
- respected
- emotionally safe

And when those feelings change...
friendships start feeling unstable very quickly.

Sometimes people pull away because they are stressed.
Sometimes because groups influence them.
Sometimes because they are insecure themselves.
And sometimes people accidentally hurt each other without realizing how strongly small moments can affect someone emotionally.

This section is not about becoming suspicious of everybody.
And it is definitely not about overthinking every text message.
It is about learning to recognize patterns.

Healthy friendships usually feel:	Confusing friendships often feel:
safe	unpredictable
relaxed	tense
honest	performative
consistent	emotionally draining
easy to be yourself inside	filled with mixed signals

Friendships are emotional ecosystems.
And once you start noticing the hidden signals underneath them...
you begin understanding people — and yourself — much more clearly.

Because sometimes friendship is not confusing because you are "bad at people."
Sometimes human emotions are simply complicated.
Especially when everybody is still figuring themselves out at the same time.

"I Was Kidding"— Or Was I?

"No, seriously... I was kidding."
Ethan laughed after saying it.
But nobody else did.
Not really.

- ★ One kid looked down at the table.
- ★ Another forced a tiny smile.
- ★ The room felt weird for a second.
  Heavy.
- ★ Ethan kept grinning like nothing happened.
- ★ But everyone could feel it:
  the joke had crossed some invisible line.

A lot of people use jokes to hide real feelings.
Sometimes they say something mean...
then quickly cover it with:

"Relax." "I'm joking." "Can't you take a joke?"

But your brain notices something important:
real jokes and hidden attacks
do not feel the same.

That's because communication is not only about words.
It's also about:

- tone
- timing
- facial expressions
- tension
- energy

Someone can say something "funny"...
while sounding angry underneath.
And people usually feel that difference immediately.

Sometimes joking is friendly.
Sometimes it's a test.
Sometimes it's a safe way to say
something someone secretly means.

That's why certain jokes make people laugh...
and other jokes make the whole room
feel uncomfortable.

Signals to Notice

	• the smile disappears too fast
	• the voice sounds sharp or cold
	• the person keeps repeating the "joke"
	• everyone laughs nervously instead of naturally
	• someone looks embarrassed afterward
	• the joker watches people's reactions very carefully
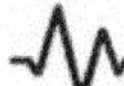	• the energy feels tense instead of fun

A real joke usually makes people feel included.
A hidden attack often makes someone feel smaller.
And sometimes the person telling the joke does not even fully realize they're doing it.

People sometimes hide honesty inside humor
because it feels safer.
Especially when they are angry.
Jealous.
Embarrassed.
Or trying to impress other people.

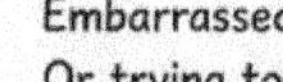

Real-Life Example

Sofia showed her drawing to
a group of kids before class.

One boy laughed and said:

"Wow... did a five-year-old make that?"

A couple kids laughed quietly.

Then he quickly added:

"I'm kidding."

But Sofia stopped smiling.
And even the kids laughing
looked uncomfortable after a second.

Why?

Because everyone could hear
the difference between playful teasing...
and embarrassment disguised as a joke.

Try This

The next time someone says:

"Relax. I'm kidding."

pause for one second and notice:

How did the room feel right before
they said that?

Awkward?

Warm?

Tense?

People often reveal their real emotions
in the tiny moment before the
"joking" begins.

Real Laughs vs. Fake Laughs

- ★ The whole table exploded laughing. At least... that's what it sounded like. But Noah noticed something strange.
- ★ Nobody kept laughing afterward. The smiles disappeared too fast.
- ★ One kid immediately looked at their phone.
- ★ Another glanced at the teacher.
- ★ And the girl who made the joke kept watching everyone's reactions instead of laughing herself.

Something felt fake about it.

Humans laugh for many different reasons.
Not all laughter means:

"That was funny."

Sometimes people laugh because they:

- feel nervous
- want to fit in
- don't know what else to do
- feel uncomfortable
- want approval from the group
- are trying to avoid awkward silence

That's one of the hidden rules of social situations:
people often laugh to manage emotions... not just because something is hilarious.

Real laughter usually feels relaxed.
Natural.
Easy.
Fake laughter often feels tighter.
Faster.
Forced.

- ★ Sometimes a person laughs while their eyes stay completely serious.
- ★ Sometimes the laugh ends too suddenly.
- ★ Sometimes everyone laughs at the same time... then instantly goes quiet again.

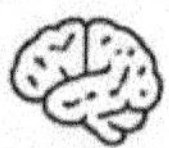

Your brain notices these tiny differences even before you can explain them.

That's why certain rooms feel warm and fun... while others feel weird even when everyone is technically "laughing."

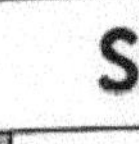

Signals to Notice

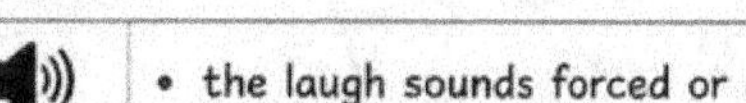

- the laugh sounds forced or extra loud
- people stop laughing very quickly
- someone looks around before laughing
- the smile does not reach the eyes
- people laugh while looking uncomfortable
- the laughter feels nervous instead of relaxed
- one person laughs much harder than everyone else

Real laughter usually spreads naturally.
Fake laughter often feels performative.
Like people are trying to show something instead of genuinely feeling it.

Real-Life Example

★ During lunch, Ava accidentally dropped her fork onto the floor.

★ One boy laughed loudly and slapped the table.

★ A few others joined in immediately.

But the laughter felt strange.
Too sharp.
Too fast.
Ava forced a smile,
but her face turned red.

Then, a second later, the entire table went quiet.

Nobody actually thought it was that funny.

They were reacting to the awkwardness.

Not the joke itself.

Try This

The next time a group laughs loudly...

watch what happens right after.

Do people stay relaxed?

Does the conversation keep flowing naturally?

Or does the energy suddenly feel tense and awkward?

Real emotions usually appear in the seconds after the laughter ends.

When a Friend Starts Pulling Away

- At first, Mia told herself she was imagining it.
- Her friend still said hi.
- Still sat near her sometimes.
- Still answered texts.
- But something had changed.
- The conversations felt shorter.
- The smiles looked smaller.
- And somehow...
- Mia always felt like she was chasing the friendship instead of relaxing inside it.

One of the hardest social signals to notice is distance that happens slowly.
Because most friendships do not end dramatically. Usually, they fade little by little.
Signal by signal.

A person who once looked excited to see you...
starts acting slightly different.
Not always mean.
Not always obvious.
Just... farther away.

Humans often struggle to say difficult things directly.
So instead of saying:

"I don't feel the same anymore."

they sometimes communicate it through behavior first.

That's why emotional distance often appears before words do.

And the confusing part is:
people pulling away are not always angry.

Sometimes they are stressed.

Focused on new friendships.

Embarrassed.

Changing.

Or dealing with something you cannot see.

Not every distant moment means rejection.
But patterns matter.
Especially repeated patterns.

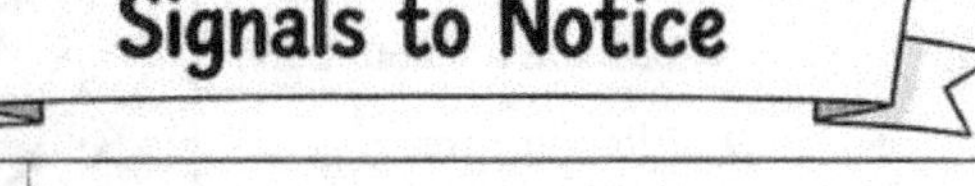

Signals to Notice

	• shorter replies than usual
	• less eye contact
	• slower responses to messages
	• canceling plans more often
	• acting different around other people
	• conversations feeling forced instead of easy
	• less curiosity about your life
	• you always being the one who reaches out first

Healthy friendships usually feel balanced.
Not perfect.
But balanced.

You should not constantly feel like you are trying to hold the friendship together alone.

Real-Life Example

- ★ Jordan and Alex used to walk home together almost every day.
- ★ They joked constantly.
- ★ Sent dumb memes late at night.
- ★ And talked about everything.

 Then little things started changing.

- Alex began walking with another group after school.
- His replies became shorter.
- Sometimes he left Jordan's messages unopened for hours.
- When they talked in person,
  Alex still sounded friendly...
  but distracted.
  Like part of him was
  somewhere else.

 Jordan kept wondering:

"Did I do something wrong?"

➡

 But the truth was more complicated.
Alex was trying hard to fit into a new group and was changing how he acted around different people.

➡

 It still hurt.
But not every friendship change has one dramatic reason.
Sometimes people slowly drift in different directions.

Try This

 The next time you feel someone pulling away...
do not focus on one moment.

 Focus on <u>patterns</u>.

 Ask yourself:

"Has the energy between us changed consistently over time?"

 Because relationships are often shaped by small repeated signals...
not one single event.

Being Included vs. Being Tolerated

The group said Olivia could sit with them.
But something felt off.

- ★ Nobody moved over to make space.
- ★ Nobody looked excited to see her.
- ★ The conversation kept going without really including her in it.
- ★ Every time she tried to speak, the group answered quickly… then moved on again.
- ★ Olivia sat there the whole lunch period feeling invisible.

Sometimes people are physically included… but emotionally kept at the edge of the group.

And humans can usually feel that difference very fast.

That's because belonging is not only about being allowed near people.
It's about how people react to your presence.

Real inclusion feels warm. Natural. Relaxed.

Being tolerated feels different. You are technically there… but the energy never fully opens toward you.

Real belonging usually feels mutual. You do not have to constantly fight for space inside the group.

That's because belonging is not only about being allowed near people.

It's about how people react to your presence.

Nobody is openly mean.
But something quietly says:
"You're not really part of this."

This happens in schools all the time.
And many kids blame themselves immediately.
But social groups are complicated.

Sometimes groups already have invisible routines and inside dynamics.

Sometimes people do not notice they are excluding someone.

And sometimes certain groups protect their "core" without saying it out loud.

The important thing is learning to notice the difference… without automatically deciding something is wrong with you.

Signals to Notice

- people rarely ask you questions back
- conversations continue around you instead of with you
- nobody saves you a seat
- the group becomes quieter when you join
- people respond politely but without much energy
- inside jokes constantly happen around you
- plans get discussed without including you naturally
- you leave feeling drained instead of relaxed

Real belonging usually feels mutual. You do not have to constantly fight for space inside the group.

Real-Life Example

Eli started sitting with a different group during science camp.

Nobody rejected him.
In fact, they always said:

"Yeah, sure, sit here."

But every conversation felt slightly closed.

The group talked mostly to each other.

When Eli made jokes, the laughs sounded quick and polite.

One afternoon, everyone started planning a weekend hangout right in front of him... without inviting him.

Nobody was cruel.
But for the first time,
Eli realized:

being allowed near people is not always the same as being welcomed by them.

Try This

The next time you are around a group, notice this:

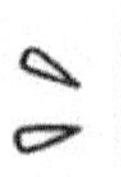

Do you feel pressure to earn your place every second?

Or do you feel relaxed enough to simply exist there?

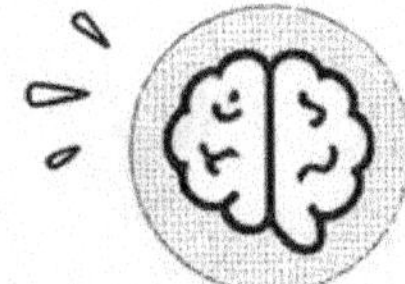

Your nervous system often notices the difference between acceptance... and tolerance... before your brain fully explains it.

The Friend Who Changes Around Other People

When Ava and Lily were alone together, everything felt normal.

They laughed constantly.
Shared secrets.
Talked like best friends.

But the second other kids showed up…
Lily became different.

- ★ Her voice changed.
- ★ She interrupted Ava more.
- ★ Acted louder.
- ★ Cooler.
- ★ Sometimes she even teased Ava in front of the group.

And afterward, Ava always felt confused.
Like she had **two different versions** of the same friend.

A lot of people change slightly depending on who they are around. That part is normal. Humans naturally adjust their behavior in different groups.

But sometimes the change becomes so strong… it makes the friendship feel unstable. Especially when someone acts warm in private… but distant or embarrassing in public.

Why does this happen?

Usually because social groups create pressure.
People often want:

approval	status	attention	protection from embarrassment	a certain image inside the group

And sometimes a person becomes so focused on fitting in… they stop acting like themselves.

That does not always mean they are fake.
Sometimes it means they are insecure.
Trying to survive socially.
Trying to avoid becoming the target themselves.

Insecure.

Trying to survive socially.

Trying to avoid becoming the target themselves.

Still, it can hurt deeply when someone treats you differently depending on who is watching.

Because consistency is one of the biggest signs of trust.

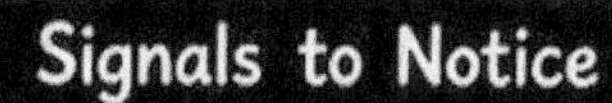

Signals to Notice

-  they act warmer alone than in groups
-  their personality changes dramatically around certain people
-  they tease you more when others are watching
-  they ignore you to impress the group
-  they suddenly copy the group's opinions
-  conversations feel less genuine in public
-  they seem worried about looking "cool"

Confident people usually stay relatively consistent.

Insecure people often shape-shift depending on the room.

Real-Life Example

Marcus and Ben had been friends for years.

During gaming nights, Ben acted relaxed and funny.

But at school, when the older soccer players were around, everything changed.

 Ben laughed harder at mean jokes.

 Pretended not to hear Marcus sometimes.

 And one day, after Marcus answered a question wrong in class, Ben smirked and said:

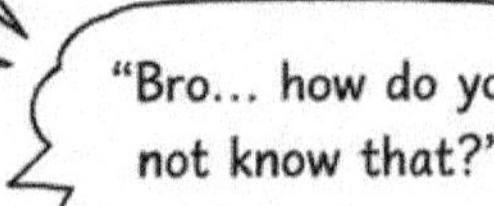

The group laughed. Marcus laughed too.

But inside, something felt different after that.

Because the joke was not really about humor. It was about Ben trying to protect his position inside the group.

Try This

The next time someone changes around other people, ask yourself:

"Who are they trying to impress right now?"

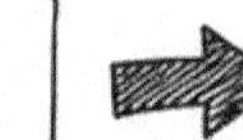

Sometimes that question explains more than the words themselves.

And pay attention to this:

How someone treats you when they have <u>social power</u> around others... often reveals who they truly are underneath.

The Joke Everyone Understands Except You

Everyone at the table laughed immediately.
Except Daniel.
He smiled half a second too late.
Because he had no idea what everyone was talking about.

The conversation moved fast after that.
Someone said:
"You had to be there."
Another kid repeated part of the joke.
Everyone laughed again.

Daniel laughed too this time…
even though he still did not understand it.

Few things feel stranger than being the only person outside a shared moment.
Especially when everybody else seems connected by something invisible.

Inside jokes are powerful social signals.

They quietly tell the group:

 "We share history."

 "We understand each other."

 "We belong together."

That's why inside jokes can feel warm and fun when you are included…
and painful when you are not.

Humans naturally form small social circles.
Shared memories become shortcuts.

A single word.
A weird nickname.
One random moment from months ago.

And suddenly everyone who was there starts laughing again.

The problem happens when someone feels excluded repeatedly.
Because after a while, they stop feeling like part of the group story.

And sometimes people fake understanding just to avoid feeling embarrassed.

 They laugh late.

 Copy other people's reactions.

 Pretend they "get it."

Most people do this at least sometimes.
Even adults.

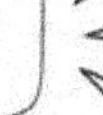

Signals to Notice

- people laugh before you understand why
-  someone says "never mind" instead of explaining
-  the group references old memories constantly
-  you feel pressure to fake a reaction
-  everyone seems emotionally connected except you
-  conversations move too fast to ask questions
-  people assume "everybody knows" something you do not

Healthy groups usually make space for people to catch up.

Unhealthy groups sometimes use inside jokes to quietly protect the group boundary.

Real-Life Example

At soccer practice,
the team kept repeating
the phrase:

"Watch out for the squirrels."

Every time someone said it,
the older kids burst out laughing.

"Watch out for the squirrels!"

Leo had joined the team only two weeks earlier.

He smiled politely every time...
but secretly felt lost.

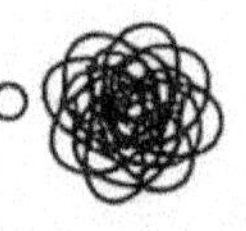

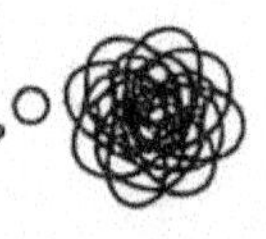

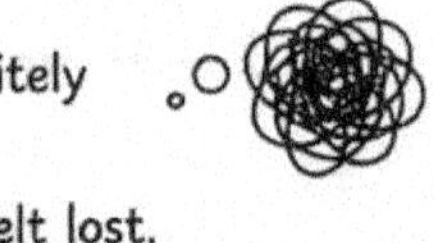

FINALLY, DURING WATER BREAK...

Months earlier, a squirrel had run across the field during an important game and completely distracted their goalkeeper.

The whole team had laughed so hard they still joked about it now.

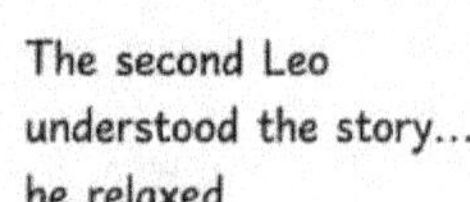

The second Leo understood the story... he relaxed.

Because suddenly the joke no longer felt like a locked door.

It felt like a shared memory he had finally been invited into.

Try This

The next time you do not understand a joke immediately...
notice your first reaction.

Do you panic?

Pretend?

Go quiet?

Or simply ask what happened?

Most people are far less bothered by explaining a joke... than by someone pretending to belong while secretly feeling disconnected.

PART V

THE HIDDEN RULES OF GROUPS

Groups have rules nobody explains out loud.
But almost everybody feels them.

You walk toward a lunch table and instantly sense:
whether people want you there.
A group starts laughing and somehow you can tell:
who feels included...
and who is pretending to feel included.

One person enters the room and suddenly everybody acts different.

- ★ Louder.
- ★ More careful.
- ★ More nervous.
- ★ More competitive.

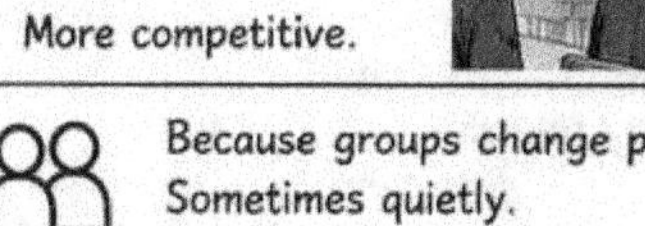

Because groups change people.
Sometimes quietly.
Sometimes dramatically.

Humans behave differently when other humans are watching.
Especially in groups.

- ★ That is why kind people sometimes join teasing.
- ★ Quiet people suddenly become louder.
- ★ Confident people start acting insecure.
- ★ And people who seem powerful alone...
  can completely change around certain groups.

Groups create invisible pressure.
Pressure to:

 fit in	 agree	 look confident
 avoid embarrassment	 protect social status	 avoid becoming the next target

Most people do not even realize how strongly groups affect their behavior.
But your brain notices it constantly.

That strange feeling when everybody starts copying one person's energy? **Group behavior.**
The way people laugh harder when others are watching? **Group behavior.**
The way one confident person can shift the mood of an entire room? **Group behavior.**

Even silence inside groups communicates things.

 Who gets interrupted.

 Who gets ignored.

 Who everyone watches before reacting.

 Who people quietly follow without questioning.

Every group develops emotional patterns over time.

Leaders	Followers	People who create tension	People who calm everyone down	People who secretly control the mood without talking the most

And one hidden truth about groups is this:
most people want belonging more than they admit.

That is why people sometimes:

- ★ copy others
- ★ hide their real opinions
- ★ laugh at jokes they dislike
- ★ stay quiet when something feels wrong
- ★ act different around different groups

Not because they are fake.
Because humans are deeply affected by social acceptance.
Especially during school years.

This section is about learning to notice the hidden rules groups create automatically.
Not to become cynical.
Not to "analyze" every friendship circle.
But to understand why groups can sometimes feel:

 safe...	 stressful...	 welcoming...	 or emotionally exhausting.

Because once you start seeing the invisible social patterns underneath group behavior...
a lot of confusing situations suddenly become easier to understand.
You realize: groups are not random.
They have emotional gravity.
And everybody inside them feels it —
even when nobody talks about it out loud.

Why Groups Sometimes Exclude Someone

Nobody told Ryan he could not join them.
But somehow...
every time he walked over, the circle felt tighter.
The conversation changed.
People answered him quickly
without really pulling him in.
Then, a few minutes later, someone would say:

"We're gonna go do something."

And Ryan would realize they meant without him.

Social exclusion is one of the oldest human behaviors in the world. And sometimes it happens without anyone saying a single mean word out loud.

That's because groups are not only collections of people.
Groups are systems.

★ They have
★ invisible rules.
★ invisible roles.
★ invisible power.

Most groups naturally protect their "inside."
Especially when people are worried about:

- status
- popularity
- fitting in
- attention
- social hierarchy
- becoming excluded themselves

Sometimes groups exclude someone on purpose.
Sometimes they barely realize they are doing it.
And sometimes one strong personality influences everybody else without saying it directly.

Humans are deeply affected by group energy.

If one person acts cold toward someone...
others often copy that behavior automatically.
Not because they are evil.
Because humans fear standing outside the group too.

That does not make exclusion harmless.
But it explains why it spreads so fast.

Signals to Notice

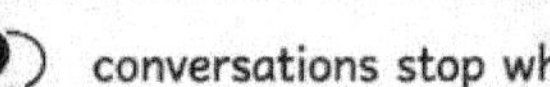

- conversations stop when someone approaches

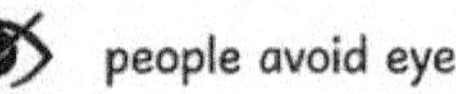

- people avoid eye contact with one person

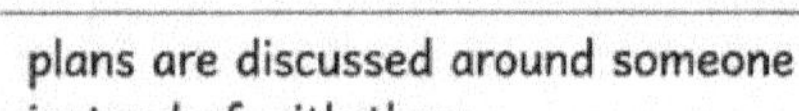

- plans are discussed around someone instead of with them

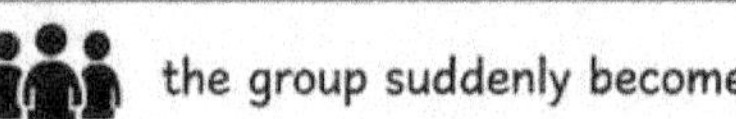

- the group suddenly becomes "full"

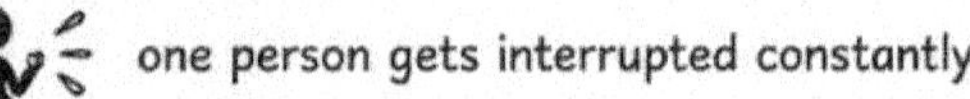

- one person gets interrupted constantly

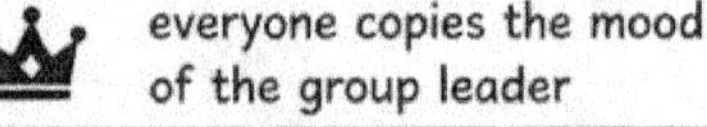

- everyone copies the mood of the group leader
- someone is physically present but emotionally ignored

Healthy groups make space.
Unhealthy groups protect status.

Very often, exclusion is less about the excluded person...
and more about the group dynamics happening underneath.

Real-Life Example

During art club, Emma noticed something strange happening to Noah.

Nobody bullied him directly.

But every time he suggested an idea, the group ignored it.

When he spoke,
people talked over him.

If he walked toward one table,
backpacks suddenly "needed space."

The weird part?
Most kids probably would have said they were being perfectly nice.

One afternoon,
a new student named Maya sat beside him and simply asked:

"Which design do you think looks better?"

It was a tiny moment.
But Noah immediately spoke more, smiled more, and looked less tense.

Because sometimes inclusion is not complicated. Sometimes it is just making someone feel visible again.

Try This

The next time you are inside a group, quietly notice:

Who gets the least attention?

Who gets interrupted most?

Who seems to be trying hardest to earn a place?

Groups reveal a lot about themselves by how they treat the person with the least social power in the room.

The Leader Everyone Quietly Follows

Nobody voted for her.
Nobody announced she was the leader.
But somehow...
everyone watched Kayla before making decisions.
If she laughed, the group relaxed.
If she looked annoyed, the whole table became quieter.
And when she stood up to leave...
half the group followed without even thinking about it.

Every group has invisible influence.
Sometimes the loudest person controls the room.
But often...
the real leader is quieter than people expect.

Because leadership is not only about talking the most.
It is about affecting the emotional direction of the group.

Humans constantly watch each other for signals.
Especially in groups.
People look for clues like:

- ★ Who seems confident?
- ★ Who gets attention naturally?
- ★ Who decides what is "cool"?
- ★ Who changes the mood when they arrive?
- ★ Who do others copy automatically?

That person often becomes the social center of the group.

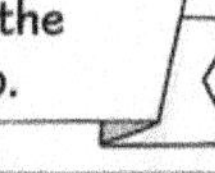

Sometimes leaders are kind and calming.
Sometimes they create drama.
And sometimes the group follows them so automatically...
nobody even realizes it is happening.

One strong personality can completely shape the emotional atmosphere of a room.
That's why certain groups suddenly become louder, meaner, calmer, or more awkward depending on one person's energy.

And sometimes the group follows them so automatically...
nobody even realizes it is happening.

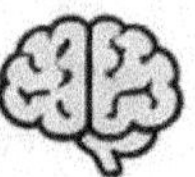

Because humans are wired to belong, they often follow without questioning.

Leadership is not about being in charge.
It is about being the person whose energy the group orbits around.

Signals to Notice

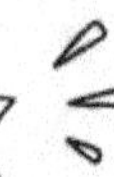

- people look at them before reacting
- others copy their opinions quickly
- conversations shift when they speak
- their approval seems unusually important
- they decide who gets attention
- the group mood changes with their mood
- people laugh harder at their jokes
- others follow their actions automatically

Real social leaders often influence the room without trying too hard.	Forced leaders usually chase attention constantly.

Real-Life Example

At summer camp, everyone thought Tyler was the "popular" kid because he talked nonstop. But Noah noticed something different.

- Whenever Emma spoke, people listened more carefully.
- When disagreements started, kids looked toward her automatically.

And one afternoon during volleyball, Tyler kept making fun of another player after a mistake.

At first, a few kids laughed nervously.

Then Emma quietly said:

- Immediately, the energy changed.
- The teasing stopped.
- People relaxed again.

That was the moment Noah realized: the real leader in a group is often the person who controls the emotional direction of everyone else.

Not necessarily the loudest voice.

Try This

The next time you are in a group, watch carefully:

Who changes the room most when they speak?

Who do people naturally watch without realizing it?

And here is the biggest clue of all:

Real influence usually looks effortless.

People follow certain leaders quietly... long before anyone says the word "leader" out loud.

The Kid Who Controls the Mood

Everything was normal until Jason walked into the room.
Then suddenly...
everyone acted different.

- ★ The table got louder.
- ★ People started trying harder to be funny.
- ★ One kid immediately began teasing someone.
- ★ Another started laughing too much.
- ★ And somehow, the entire energy of the group shifted in less than thirty seconds.

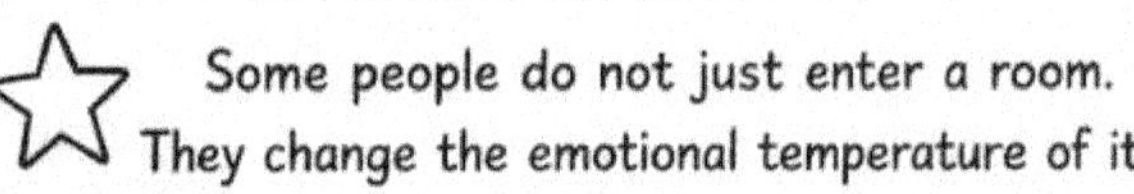

Some people do not just enter a room. They change the emotional temperature of it.

Every group has certain people who strongly affect the mood around them.

- Not always because they are the nicest.
- Or the loudest.
- Or the most popular.
- Sometimes it happens because people react emotionally to them very strongly.

Humans constantly influence each other's emotions without realizing it.

One nervous person can make everyone tense.

One calm person can make the whole group relax.

One dramatic person can pull attention toward conflict all day long.

That's why certain kids seem to control the emotional weather of a group.

When they are happy, everyone feels lighter.	When they are angry, the room feels stressful.	When they get bored, people suddenly start creating chaos.	And most groups slowly adjust themselves around that person's emotional energy.

Signals to Notice

- the room changes when they arrive
- people act differently around them
- others copy their emotional reactions
- conversations become louder or quieter instantly
- tension rises when they seem annoyed
- people try harder to impress them
- the group follows their emotional energy automatically
- everyone seems relieved when they are in a good mood

Emotion spreads through groups faster than most people realize. Especially strong emotions.

Real-Life Example

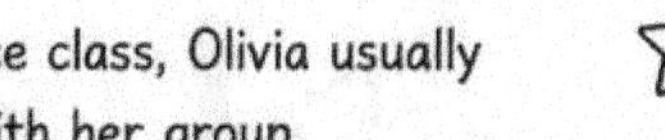
During science class, Olivia usually sat quietly with her group.

Everyone stayed focused.

The conversations felt relaxed.

Then Marcus joined their table for a project one afternoon.

Within minutes, everything changed.

People stopped paying attention. The group became louder.

Marcus kept making jokes and pushing people's buttons to get reactions.

Whenever he laughed, others laughed too — even when the jokes were not very funny.

By the end of class, almost nobody had finished the assignment.

Walking out of the room, Olivia realized something strange:

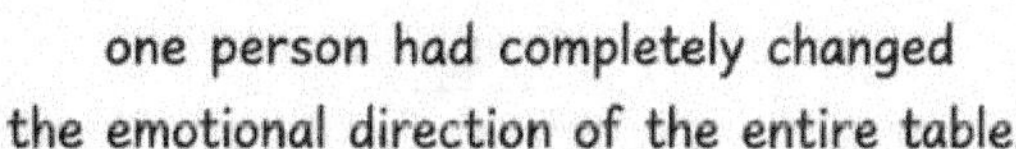
one person had completely changed the emotional direction of the entire table.

Try This

The next time you are in a group, notice this:

- Who affects the room most emotionally?
- Who makes people calmer?
- Who makes people nervous?
- Who creates chaos?

And ask yourself something even more important:

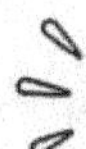
When you spend time around certain people... do you usually leave feeling better... or more exhausted than before?

Feeling Invisible in a Group

The conversation kept moving around Chloe...
without ever really reaching her.
People talked across her.
Around her.
Over her.
Every time she tried to say something,
the moment disappeared before she could enter it.
So eventually...
she stopped trying.

One of the loneliest feelings in the world is being surrounded by people... while feeling emotionally unseen.

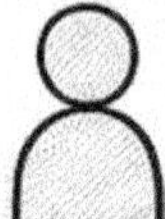

Because invisibility in groups is usually quiet.
Nobody points at you and says:
"You don't matter."
Instead, it happens through tiny moments:

- ✖ not being noticed.
- ✖ Not being included.
- ✖ Not being reacted to.

Human brains are extremely sensitive to attention.
We constantly look for signals like:

- Are people listening to me?
- Do my words affect the group?
- Does my presence change anything?
- Would anyone notice if I left?

When the answer keeps feeling like "no"... people slowly begin shrinking themselves.

- Talking less.
- Taking up less space.
- Expecting less attention.

And the dangerous part is: after enough time, invisibility can start feeling normal.

But being quiet does not mean being unimportant.
And groups often overlook people for reasons that have nothing to do with value.

Sometimes louder personalities dominate the space.

Sometimes fast conversations leave quieter people behind.

Sometimes groups accidentally create invisible social rankings without realizing it.

Signals to Notice

- ★ people interrupt you constantly
- ★ nobody reacts much when you speak
- ★ conversations continue without acknowledging your comments
- ★ people forget you are there physically
- ★ your ideas get noticed only after someone else repeats them
- ★ you feel emotionally tired after group conversations
- ★ you spend more time observing than participating
- ★ you hesitate before speaking because you expect not to be heard

Healthy groups create openings for quieter people too.
Not just the loudest voices.

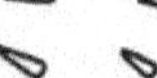

Real-Life Example

 During a history project, four students sat around one table planning ideas.

 Every time Mia suggested something, the conversation skipped past it.

 Then ten minutes later, another student repeated almost the exact same idea.

 This time, everyone loved it.

 Mia smiled politely...
but inside, she felt herself disappearing more with every minute.

 Near the end of class, the teacher walked by and asked:
"Whose idea was the timeline design?"

 One student pointed toward Mia.

 And suddenly, for the first time that day, the group actually looked at her.
Really looked at her.

 Sometimes invisibility breaks in one small moment of recognition.

Try This

The next time you are in a group, quietly notice:

- Who gets talked over most?
- Who seems to give up trying to enter the conversation?

And if you notice someone fading into the background...
try doing one simple thing:

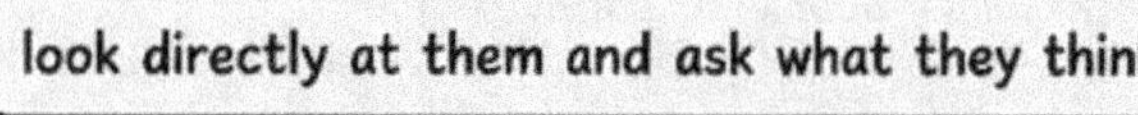
look directly at them and ask what they think.

That tiny moment can completely change how visible a person feels inside a group.

Spotting Fake Confidence

Dylan acted confident all the time. Too confident.

He talked over people constantly.

Laughed the loudest in the room.

 Made fun of anyone who looked nervous.

 And somehow... everything about him felt like he was performing instead of relaxing.

 A lot of people think confidence looks loud. But real confidence and fake confidence often feel completely different.

 Real confidence usually feels calm. Steady. Comfortable.

 Fake confidence often feels forced. Like someone is trying very hard to prove something.

That's because insecurity sometimes hides itself behind big energy.

Humans do this more than people realize.

Some people become:

- extra loud
- overly competitive
- constantly sarcastic
- attention-seeking
- controlling
- obsessed with looking "cool"

not because they feel strong inside...
but because they are **afraid of looking weak.**

 Real confidence does not panic when attention moves away.

 Fake confidence often needs constant reactions from other people to survive.

 And strangely enough...
people can usually feel the difference.
Even if they cannot explain it.

Signals to Notice

 they interrupt constantly

 they brag too much

 they need attention all the time

 they make others look smaller to feel bigger

 they cannot laugh at themselves

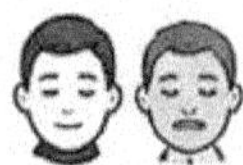 they change personality depending on the audience

 they act confident but react badly to tiny criticism

 their energy feels tense instead of relaxed

 Real confidence usually makes other people feel comfortable.

 Fake confidence often makes the room feel exhausting.

Real-Life Example

 At basketball camp, Connor acted fearless around everyone.

 He talked like he was the best player there.

 If someone missed a shot, he joked about it immediately.

 During drills, he kept trying difficult moves just to impress the group.

 But one afternoon, the coach corrected him in front of everyone.

 Only one small comment.

 And suddenly Connor's whole mood changed.

 He became defensive.

 Quiet.

 Annoyed at everybody.

 That was the moment Ethan realized: people who are truly confident usually do not fall apart from one little hit to their ego.

Try This

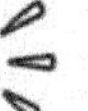

The next time someone seems "super confident," notice this:

 Do they make the people around them feel relaxed...

or nervous?

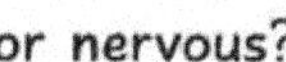

 Because real confidence rarely needs to dominate the room.

 Very often, the strongest people are the ones who no longer need to constantly prove they are strong.

Why People Act Different Around Friends

Kayden barely recognized his cousin at school.
At home, Marcus was relaxed.
Funny.
Normal.
But around his friends?
Everything changed.

★ His voice got louder.
★ He acted tougher.
★ Started using words he never used at home.
★ And laughed at things that normally did not even seem funny to him.

It felt like watching someone switch personalities.

Humans change around groups more than they realize. Especially during school years.

Because people are constantly asking themselves invisible questions like:

- Do I fit in here?
- What version of me do these people like most?
- What makes me look confident?
- What will make me accepted?

Most people adjust their behavior slightly depending on the group they are in.

That part is normal.
You probably act a little different with:

family

close friends

teachers

teammates

strangers

But sometimes the change becomes much bigger.

Especially when someone feels pressure to protect their social position.

That's when people start performing instead of relaxing.

They copy the energy of the group.
The humor.
The attitude.
Even the opinions.
Sometimes without fully realizing it.

That's why kind people can suddenly become meaner around certain friends.
Or quiet people become louder.
Or confident people suddenly become nervous.

Groups affect behavior powerfully.
Much more powerfully than most people understand.

Signals to Notice

★ their personality changes fast around certain people
★ their voice or energy becomes completely different
★ they suddenly copy the group's behavior
★ they act tougher, louder, or meaner in groups
★ they seem more focused on approval than connection
★ they treat different people differently depending on who is watching
★ they look more relaxed one-on-one than in groups

The more insecure someone feels socially... the more dramatically they often change depending on the room.

Real-Life Example

Sophie loved hanging out with Emma after school.

Emma was thoughtful.

Easy to talk to.

But during lunch, when a certain group sat nearby, Emma became almost unrecognizable.

- ★ She interrupted more.
- ★ Rolled her eyes at people.
- ★ Pretended not to care about things she normally cared about.

One afternoon, Sophie asked her:

"Why do you act so different around them?"

Emma shrugged immediately.

"I don't."

But the truth was...

she did.

And deep down, she probably knew it too.

♥ Because sometimes people slowly shape themselves around a group without noticing how far they are drifting from who they actually are.

Try This

The next time someone changes around friends, notice this:

Do they seem more relaxed... or more performative?

More real... or more controlled?

☆ The people who know who they are usually stay fairly consistent in different rooms.

But people still searching for approval often change themselves depending on who is watching.

PART VI

TOUGH MOMENTS & SOCIAL PRESSURE

Some social moments feel heavy instantly.
A joke goes too far.
The room suddenly gets quiet.
Someone says:

"Relax. It's not a big deal."

But your stomach tightens anyway.

Because humans are extremely sensitive to social pressure.
Especially in groups.
Especially when emotions rise fast.

One awkward moment can suddenly make your brain start racing:

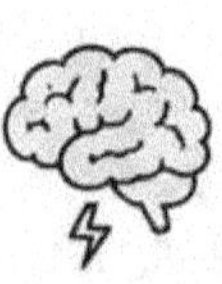

- ★ What do I say?
- ★ Is everyone watching me?
- ★ Do they think I'm weak?
- ★ Should I laugh?
- ★ Should I defend myself?
- ★ Should I stay quiet?

That pressure can feel overwhelming.
And the strange part is:
people often react emotionally before they even think clearly.

- Someone embarrassed may become angry.
- Someone nervous may start laughing.
- Someone hurt may pretend not to care.
- Someone feeling attacked may suddenly go silent.

The body reacts fast during stressful social moments.

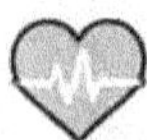

Heart racing.

Voice changing.

Face heating up.

Thoughts moving too quickly.

That is why difficult social situations often become messy.
Not because people are evil.
Because emotions affect behavior powerfully.

Especially when:

- ★ groups are watching
- ★ someone feels embarrassed
- ★ social status feels threatened
- ★ people want reactions
- ★ nobody wants to look weak

Some people respond to pressure by exploding.

Others completely shut down.

But emotionally strong people usually learn something different:
staying calm gives you power.

Not fake calm.
Real calm.
The kind that helps you think clearly while everybody else is reacting emotionally.

Because one hidden social rule is this:
people often lose control when emotions become stronger than awareness.

That is why:

- ⚠ teasing can suddenly become bullying.
- ⚠ arguments escalate fast.
- ⚠ group pressure makes good people act differently.
- ⚠ and why silence can sometimes feel louder than yelling.

This section is about understanding difficult social moments without panicking inside them.
Learning to notice:

- ★ when someone wants a reaction from you
- ★ when tension is rising
- ★ when teasing becomes harmful
- ★ when a calm voice is not actually calm
- ★ when somebody feels uncomfortable
- ★ how to protect your boundaries without creating chaos

One important truth about confidence is this:

real confidence is usually quieter than people expect.
It does not need to scream.
It does not need to dominate the room.

Sometimes the strongest person in the room is simply the one who stays emotionally steady while everybody else loses control.

And once you start understanding how social pressure affects people...
difficult moments stop feeling so mysterious.
You begin seeing the emotional patterns underneath them.
And that awareness changes everything.

The Silence That Feels Heavy

Nobody was talking anymore.
But somehow...
the room felt louder than before.

 Ava stared at her tray.

 Two kids avoided eye contact.

 Someone tapped their fingers against the table nervously.

 And across the room, a chair scraped against the floor way too loudly.

 Nobody said:
"This is awkward."
Nobody had to.
Everyone could feel it.

 Some silences feel peaceful.
Others feel heavy.
Tense.
Sharp.
Like something invisible is sitting in the middle of the room.

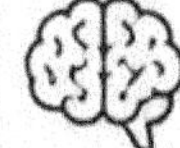 Humans are extremely sensitive to emotional tension.
Even when nobody explains what is wrong.
Your brain constantly scans for signals like:

- facial expressions
- eye contact
- posture
- tone changes
- sudden quietness
- nervous movements

 That's why certain silences instantly make people uncomfortable.

 Usually, heavy silence appears after something emotional happens.

 A rude comment.

 An argument.

 An embarrassing moment.

 A joke that went too far.

 Or sometimes...
a feeling nobody wants to talk about directly.

 And the strange part is:
people often start acting differently before they even consciously understand why the room feels tense.

Someone laughs nervously.

Another person suddenly checks their phone.

Someone changes the subject too quickly.

 Humans try to escape emotional discomfort fast.
Especially in groups.

Signals to Notice

- people avoiding eye contact
- nervous laughter
- sudden quiet after loud conversation
- stiff body language
- forced smiles
- people pretending to be busy
- quick subject changes
- tiny sounds suddenly feeling very noticeable

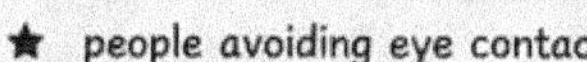

 Heavy silence usually means emotions are being felt...
but not openly discussed.

Real-Life Example

During group work,
Liam made a joke about
Noah's presentation mistake.

At first, a couple kids
laughed automatically.

Then Noah stopped smiling.

The room went quiet
immediately afterward.
Not calm quiet.
Heavy quiet.

One student started
flipping through papers
too fast.

Another stared at
the whiteboard.

Even Liam suddenly
looked uncomfortable.

Because everybody could feel the emotional shift the second the joke stopped feeling funny. Nobody wanted to say it out loud.
But **the silence already said it.**

Try This

The next time a room suddenly becomes quiet, do not only notice the silence itself.

Notice what people start doing inside the silence.

Who looks nervous?

Who avoids looking at someone?

Who tries to escape the tension by joking or changing the subject?

Sometimes silence communicates emotions more clearly than words ever could.

Calm Voices That Aren't Calm

Dad said it quietly.
Very quietly.
But Eli immediately stopped talking.
Because even though the words sounded calm...
the room suddenly felt dangerous.

A lot of people think anger always looks loud.
Yelling.
Slamming doors.
Big reactions.
But some of the strongest emotions come out in very controlled voices.

Cold voices.

Tight voices.

Voices that sound calm on the surface...

...while tension leaks out underneath.

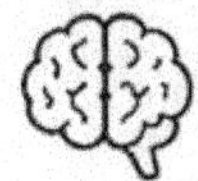

Humans are extremely sensitive to emotional contradictions.
Your brain notices when:

- the words sound calm

- the energy feels intense

That's why certain calm voices make people instantly nervous.
Even before they consciously understand why.

Sometimes people lower their voice when they are trying hard to control anger.

Sometimes they become extra calm because they want power over the situation.

And sometimes quiet tension feels scarier than shouting... because everybody senses emotion being held back.

That is one of the hidden rules of communication:
people react more to emotional energy than to words alone.

Signals to Notice

- the voice becomes unusually quiet

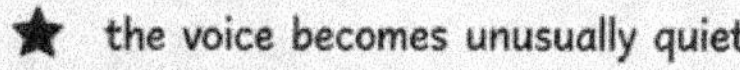

- words sound controlled instead of relaxed

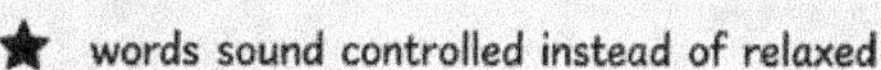

- pauses feel sharp or tense
- facial expressions stop matching the words
- eye contact feels intense
- movements become stiff or overly controlled
- the room suddenly feels emotionally smaller
- everyone becomes careful very quickly

True calm usually makes people feel safer.

Controlled anger often makes people feel more nervous.

Real-Life Example

During basketball practice, Coach Ramirez rarely yelled.

That was why the team became extra nervous when he got quiet.

One afternoon, two players kept joking around during drills.

Finally, Coach Ramirez walked over and said softly:

"Sit down for a minute."

That was it.
No shouting.
No dramatic speech.

But the entire gym became silent immediately.

Because everyone could feel the frustration underneath the calm voice.
And somehow...
that quiet disappointment felt heavier than yelling would have.

Try This

The next time someone sounds "calm," ask yourself:

Does the room feel calmer too?

OR

Or more tense?

Because real calm usually spreads safety.

But controlled anger often spreads pressure... even when the voice never gets loud.

When Someone Wants a Reaction From You

Tyler grinned across the table.
Then he said something even more annoying.
And immediately looked up to watch Noah's face.

Not the words.
The reaction.

★ Some people are not trying to start a conversation. They are trying to create an emotional response. Humans do this all the time. Especially in groups.

★ Sometimes people want:
- attention
- control
- entertainment
- validation from others
- proof they can affect you emotionally

★ That's why certain people tease, provoke, interrupt, or push buttons repeatedly. The reaction becomes the reward. And the bigger the emotional reaction… the more powerful they feel.

This does not always come from cruelty. Sometimes people are bored. Immature. Insecure. Trying to impress others. Or testing social boundaries.

But one hidden social rule stays true: people often repeat behaviors that successfully get reactions.

That's why reacting emotionally can sometimes accidentally encourage the behavior to continue. Especially in group settings.

Signals to Notice

they keep watching your face closely

they repeat the behavior after getting a reaction

they smirk before or after saying something

they seem entertained by your frustration

they act differently when other people are watching

they escalate when you react emotionally

they lose interest when reactions disappear

A lot of social power comes from emotional control.

Not pretending not to care.
But deciding what deserves your energy.

Real-Life Example

During lunch, Carter kept flicking paper pieces at Maya from across the table.

Every time she reacted, he laughed harder.

Soon other kids started watching too.

Finally, Maya stopped snapping back at him.

She turned toward her friend and continued her conversation normally.

At first, Carter tried again. Then again.

But without the reaction, the whole thing suddenly looked less funny.

Within minutes, he stopped.

Because sometimes people are not chasing conflict. They are chasing emotional impact.

Try This

The next time someone seems to be pushing your buttons, pause before reacting immediately.

Ask yourself:

"Are they trying to communicate something... or are they trying to control the emotional energy of the moment?"

Sometimes the strongest response is not giving someone the emotional performance they were hoping to get from you.

Teasing, Joking, or Bullying?

At first, everyone laughed.
Even Lucas.
The joke seemed harmless.

But then it kept happening.
Every day.
The same comments.
The same smirks.
The same people watching his reaction.

And eventually, Lucas stopped laughing too.

Sometimes it is hard to tell the difference between teasing, joking, and bullying.
Because all three can include laughter.
All three can include sarcasm.
And all three can sound similar on the surface.
But underneath...
they *feel* very different.

Friendly teasing usually feels balanced.
Safe.
Both people can laugh.
Nobody feels trapped or humiliated afterward.

Bullying feels different.
Bullying usually creates fear, embarrassment, or emotional pressure.
Especially when one person keeps becoming the target over and over again.

One of the biggest clues is this:
Does the interaction make someone feel included... or smaller?

Healthy joking usually strengthens connection.

Bullying usually strengthens power.

That is why certain "jokes" slowly make people quieter over time.
Humans often pretend things do not hurt because they do not want to seem weak.
Especially in front of groups.
So someone may laugh on the outside...
while feeling miserable inside.

Signals to Notice

one person is always the target

the "jokes" continue after someone looks uncomfortable

people laugh nervously instead of naturally

the teasing becomes harsher in groups

someone tries to escape or go quiet

the person teasing wants an audience

the behavior repeats constantly

the target looks tense even before the teasing starts

Real joking usually has mutual trust underneath it.

Bullying usually has imbalance underneath it.

Real-Life Example

Every day before math class, a group of boys joked about Ethan's backpack.

At first, Ethan laughed along. But the comments slowly got meaner.

Soon they started grabbing the backpack and tossing it between desks.

Relax. We're joking.

Whenever Ethan got upset, one boy immediately said: "Relax. We're joking."

But Ethan stopped smiling around them completely.

One afternoon, another student named Caleb quietly handed Ethan his backpack and said: "Dude... they're not joking anymore."

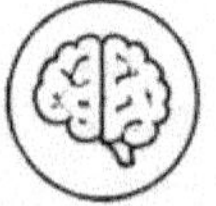

And deep down, Ethan already knew that.

Because your nervous system often recognizes bullying before your brain fully admits it.

Soon they started grabbing the backpack and tossing it between desks.

Whenever Ethan got upset, one boy immediately said:

Relax. We're joking.

But Ethan stopped smiling around them completely.

One afternoon, another student named Caleb quietly handed Ethan his backpack and said:

And deep down, Ethan already knew that. Because your nervous system often recognizes bullying before your brain fully admits it.

Try This

The next time people are "joking" around someone, watch carefully:

Is everyone genuinely having fun?

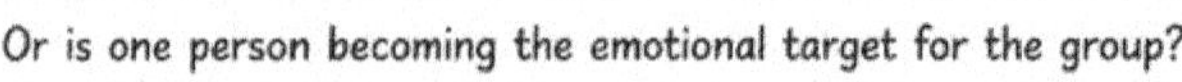

Or is one person becoming the emotional target for the group?

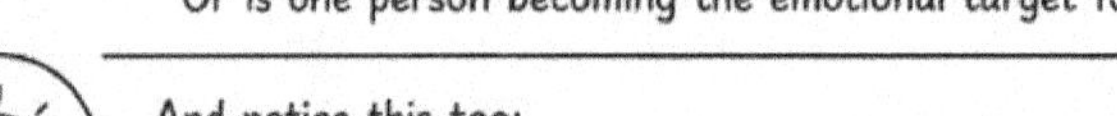

And notice this too:

If the teasing stopped completely tomorrow... would the targeted person feel relieved?

That answer usually tells you a lot.

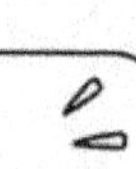

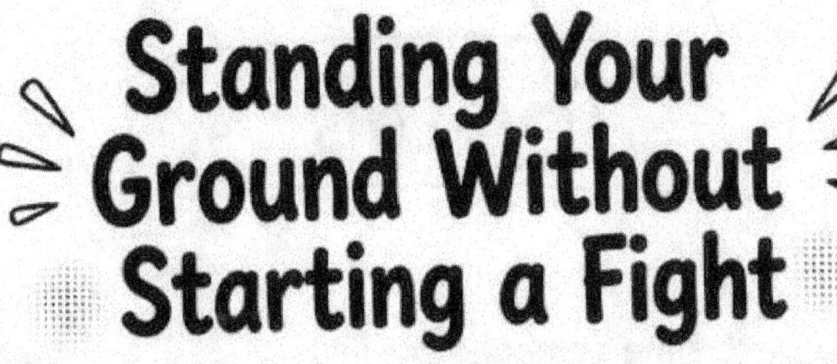

Standing Your Ground Without Starting a Fight

The whole group looked at Noah waiting for his reaction.
Someone had just made another joke at his expense.
Not a huge one.
But enough.

Noah could feel two choices fighting inside him:

explode...

or

stay completely quiet.

A lot of people think standing up for yourself means becoming aggressive.
But real confidence usually looks calmer than people expect.

Because the goal is not to "win" the moment.
The goal is to protect your boundaries without losing control of yourself.
That can be hard.
Especially when emotions rise fast.

When people feel embarrassed, attacked, or cornered, the brain often pushes toward two extremes:

fighting

or

shutting down

But there is a third option: steady confidence.

Calm.

Clear.

Direct.

People who stand their ground well usually do not over-explain.
They do not panic.
And they do not need to create a huge scene to communicate:

"That's not okay with me."

One strong sentence said calmly often carries more power than yelling.

Signals to Notice

- someone keeps testing your reaction
- the group is watching what you will do
- your body suddenly feels tense or hot
- people act stronger when they think you will stay quiet
- the energy becomes about power instead of connection
- someone backs off when you respond calmly
- people seem surprised when you stay composed

Emotional control is not weakness.
Very often, it is strength.

Real-Life Example

During lunch, Tyler grabbed Noah's notebook and held it out of reach while everyone laughed.

Normally, Noah either snapped angrily...
or pretended not to care.
But this time he stayed calm.
He looked directly at Tyler and said:

No yelling.

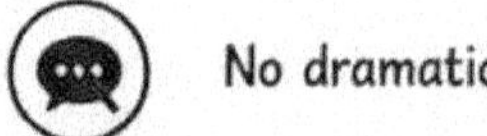
No dramatic speech.

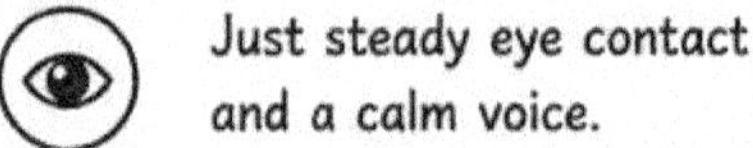
Just steady eye contact and a calm voice.

The table became quieter almost immediately.
Tyler smirked for another second...
then handed the notebook back.

Because sometimes people keep pushing until they feel resistance.
Not explosive resistance.
Confident resistance.

Try This

The next time someone pushes your boundaries, practice saying one short sentence calmly:

"Not cool."

"Cut it out."

"Give it back."

"I said no."

No long speech.
No performance.
Just clear energy.

People often expect either anger or silence.

Calm confidence surprises them more than both.

How to Tell When Someone Feels Uncomfortable

- ★ She stopped making eye contact.
- ★ Her smile became smaller.
- ★ And every time the conversation returned to her, she quietly tried to change the subject.

Most people do not directly announce when they feel uncomfortable.
Especially in groups.

Instead, the body often starts communicating it first.
Humans are constantly sending emotional signals without realizing it.
Tiny changes.
Tiny reactions.
Tiny escapes.

That's because discomfort affects the nervous system almost immediately.
And the body usually reveals it before the words do.

Discomfort often appears first in body language... before words ever explain it.

Humans are constantly sending emotional signals without realizing it.
Tiny changes.
Tiny reactions.
Tiny escapes.

Someone uncomfortable might:

- laugh too quickly

- go unusually quiet

- avoid eye contact

- cross their arms tightly

- fake-smile

- look toward exits

- shrink their posture

- fidget constantly

- try to leave the conversation

☆ One hidden social skill is learning to notice these signals early.
Not to judge people.
Not to "analyze" everybody.
But to recognize when someone may no longer feel safe, relaxed, or included.

Because socially aware people pay attention to comfort levels.
Not just conversations.

Signals to Notice

- forced or nervous laughter
- stiff body language
- shorter answers than usual
- fake smiles that disappear quickly
- avoiding eye contact
- glancing around the room often
- backing away physically
- sudden quietness after being teased or pressured
- touching the face, neck, or arms repeatedly

Real-Life Example

During a birthday party, a group of kids started teasing Jonah about a video he had posted online.

At first, Jonah laughed along. But after a few minutes, Mia noticed small changes.

Jonah's smile kept disappearing faster.

He stopped adding to the conversation.

And every time somebody brought the video up again, he looked toward the door for a second.

Finally, Mia changed the subject completely and started asking Jonah about basketball instead. Almost instantly, his shoulders relaxed again.

Because sometimes the kindest social skill is noticing discomfort before someone has to ask for help.

Try This

The next time you are talking with someone, pay attention to this:

1. Does their body seem more relaxed over time... or more closed off?

2. Do they lean into the conversation... or slowly try to escape it?

3. People often tell you how comfortable they feel... without saying a single word out loud.

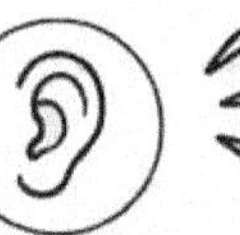

Notice the tiny signals.
They speak the loudest.
You just have to be paying attention.

PART VII

BECOMING SOMEONE PEOPLE TRUST

Some people make others feel safe almost immediately.
Not because they are the loudest.
Not because they are the most popular.
And not because they always say the "perfect" thing.
It is something else.

When they talk to you, you feel listened to.

When you make a mistake, they do not make the moment worse.

When tension appears, they calm the room instead of adding more chaos.

People trust them emotionally.
That kind of trust is powerful.
Because humans remember how other people make them feel.
More than perfect words.
More than impressiveness.
More than trying too hard to look cool.

A lot of people think trust comes from confidence alone. But real trust usually comes from emotional consistency.

People trust someone when:

- ★ their words match their actions
- ★ they stay calm under pressure
- ★ they listen without making everything about themselves
- ★ they do not humiliate others for mistakes
- ★ they feel honest instead of performative

That is why some people naturally attract friendships, respect, and leadership without forcing it.
Others feel emotionally safe around them.

And one strange truth about communication is this:

people often decide whether they trust you before they fully explain why.

Your tone matters.

Your reactions matter.

Your body language matters.

The emotional energy you bring into conversations matters.

Even small moments shape trust.

Someone drops something and everybody laughs.
One person helps instead.
Trust grows.

A friend admits they feel embarrassed.
One person listens seriously instead of turning it into a joke.
Trust grows.

Someone says sorry clearly without making excuses.
Trust grows.

Humans feel safer around people who make difficult emotions feel manageable instead of dangerous.

That does not mean becoming perfect.
Nobody is calm all the time.
Nobody handles every social situation perfectly.

But emotionally trustworthy people usually create the same feeling over and over:

"You can relax around me."

This section is about becoming that kind of person.
Not fake nice.
Not overly serious.
And definitely not someone who tries to "control" everybody emotionally.

Real trust feels natural.
Steady.
Clear.

Because socially intelligent people understand something important:

every interaction either increases safety... or increases tension.

And the people others remember most positively are often not the funniest, loudest, or coolest people in the room. They are the people who make others feel understood, respected, and emotionally safe to be human around.

That is real social intelligence.
And once you understand it...
you start affecting rooms differently without even trying.

Listening So People Feel Heard

Mason stopped talking halfway through his story.
Not because he forgot what to say.
Because he could tell nobody was really listening.
One friend kept checking his phone.
Another interrupted every few seconds.
Someone else nodded without even looking at him.
So eventually...
Mason just shrugged and said:

"Never mind."

A lot of people hear words.
Far fewer people make others feel heard.
And humans notice the difference immediately.

Real listening is not just staying quiet while waiting for your turn to talk.
It is showing someone:

"I'm actually with you right now."

That feeling matters more than most people realize.

Because when people feel truly heard, they usually become:

- calmer
- more open
- more honest
- more connected
- less defensive

That's why strong communicators often listen differently than everybody else.

They notice emotional signals.
Not just sentences.
They pay attention to:

-  tone
-  pauses
-  facial expressions
-  energy shifts
-  emotions underneath the words

And strangely enough...

people often remember how you listened to them more than what you actually said.

SIGNALS TO NOTICE

-  they stop talking when interrupted too much
-  their energy changes when someone truly listens
-  they relax when they feel understood
-  eye contact becomes more natural
-  conversations feel slower and safer
-  people share more when they feel emotionally accepted
-  distracted listening makes people shut down quickly

Listening is one of the fastest ways to make someone feel visible.

REAL-LIFE EXAMPLE

During art class, Zoe quietly told her friend Emma that her parents had been arguing a lot lately.

At first, Emma almost interrupted with advice.

But then she stopped herself.
Instead, she listened.
Really listened.

She looked at Zoe.

Asked small questions.

Did not rush the conversation.

Did not immediately try to "fix" everything.

After a minute, Zoe's whole posture changed.

- ✓ Her shoulders relaxed.
- ✓ Her voice became steadier.

Walking home later, Zoe realized something important:

- ★ Emma had not solved the problem.
- ★ But somehow, she had made Zoe feel less alone inside it.

TRY THIS

The next time someone talks to you about something important, practice this:

Do not immediately jump in with your own story.

Do not rush to fix the situation.

First, focus compeltely on understanding them.

Sometimes the most powerful thing you can give another person...
is the feeling that their thoughts actually reached somebody.

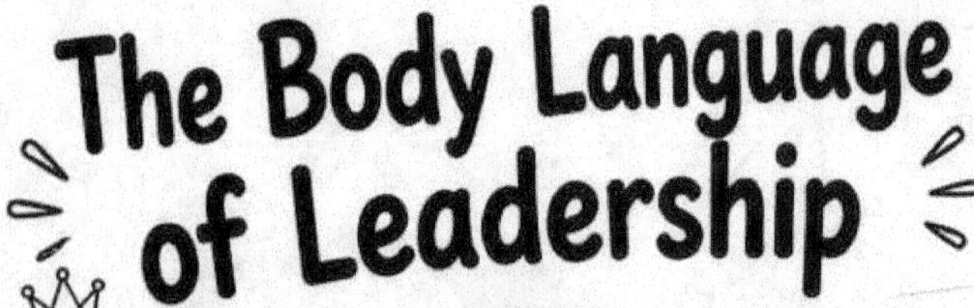

The Body Language of Leadership

When Mrs. Carter left the classroom for five minutes,
the room changed instantly.
Some kids got louder.
A few started throwing paper.
One table almost turned into complete chaos.
But in the middle of all of it, Maya stayed calm.
She did not yell.
Did not threaten anybody.
Did not try to control the room.
And somehow...
people around her naturally settled down anyway.

A lot of people imagine leaders as loud, powerful, or intimidating.
But real leadership often looks much quieter than that.

Because leadership is not only about being noticed.
It is about making other people feel stable around you.

Humans constantly read body language to decide:

-  Who seems calm under pressure?
-  Who feels emotionally steady?
-  Who reacts without panicking?
- Who makes the group feel safer?

That's why confident leaders usually move differently.
Not dramatically.
Just steadily.

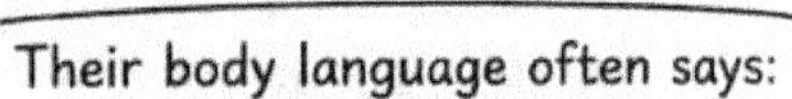

Their body language often says:

"I'm okay."

And that feeling spreads to other people.

Real leaders usually do not waste energy trying to prove they are important.
They do not need attention every second.
And they rarely create unnecessary chaos to feel powerful.

Instead, they often communicate leadership through small signals:

-  calm posture
-  relaxed movements
-  steady eye contact
-  patient listening
-  controlled reactions
-  giving others space to speak
-  staying composed during stressful moments

People trust calm energy more than forced dominance.

SIGNALS TO NOTICE

-  they stay steady when others panic
-  people naturally listen when they speak
-  they do not interrupt constantly
-  their movements look relaxed instead of frantic
-  they make others feel included
-  they stay emotionally controlled during tension
-  they listen before reacting
-  people seem calmer around them

Strong leadership often feels safe...
not scary.

REAL-LIFE EXAMPLE

During a group presentation,
the projector suddenly stopped working.
Immediately, several students panicked.

One person blamed the teacher.

Another started complaining loudly.

But Noah quietly stepped forward and said:

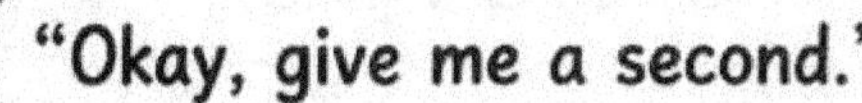

"Okay, give me a second."

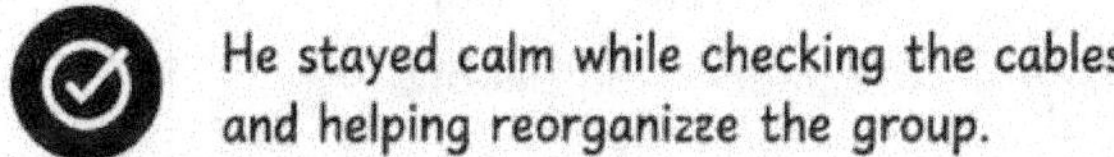

He stayed calm while checking the cables and helping reorganizze the group.

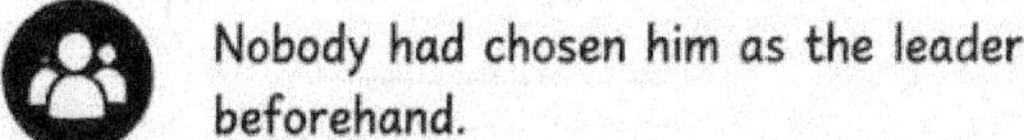

Nobody had chosen him as the leader beforehand.

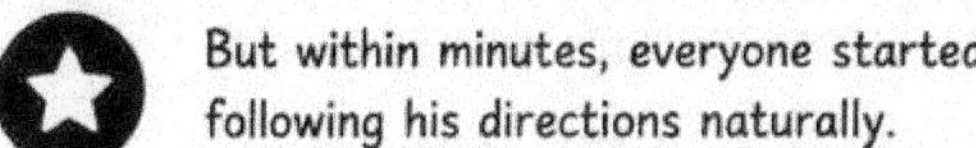

But within minutes, everyone started following his directions naturally.

Not because he acted superior.

Because his calm behavior made the group feel less overwhelmed.

That is one of the hidden truths about leadership:
people often trust the person who seems emotionally steady during stressful moments.

TRY THIS

The next time something stressful happens in a group, notice this:

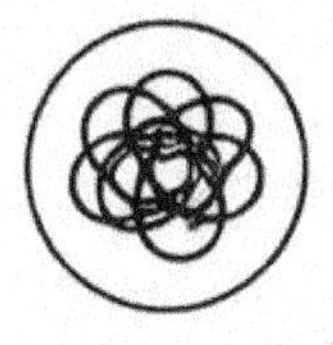

Who spreads panic?

VS.

And who spreads calm?

Because leadership is not always about controlling people.
Very often...
it is about controlling <u>your own emotional energy first.</u>

The Power of Making Others Feel Safe

Most people relaxed around Hannah
without even realizing why.
She was not the loudest person in the group.
Not the funniest either.
But somehow...
people opened up around her faster.
They smiled more.
Talked more honestly.
And seemed less nervous when she was there.

Some people make others feel judged.
Other people make others feel safe.
And that difference changes almost every social interaction.

Humans constantly ask invisible emotional questions around each other:

-  Am I being mocked right now?
-  Will this person embarrass me?
-  Is it safe to make mistakes here?
-  Can I relax around them?

Your nervous system notices those answers very quickly.

That's why emotionally safe people often become deeply trusted without trying too hard.

Because safety changes behavior.

When people feel emotionally safe, they usually:

-  speak more honestly
-  laugh more naturally
-  stop performing so much
-  become less defensive
-  show more of their real personality

And strangely enough...
making people feel safe is one of the strongest forms of social power.

Not controlling people.
Not impressing people.
Helping people relax enough to become themselves.

SIGNALS TO NOTICE

-  people seem calmer around them
-  others open up naturally
-  they do not embarrass people for mistakes
-  they listen without rushing to judge
-  nervous people relax near them
-  they stay emotionally steady during awkward moments
-  people trust them with personal things
-  conversations feel easier instead of stressful

Emotionally safe people do not need to dominate the room.
Their presence already changes the room.

Real-Life Example

During science class, Liam accidentally spilled water across the project table.

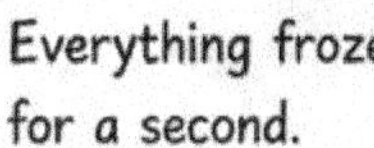

Everything froze for a second.

He looked embarrassed immediately.

A couple kids started laughing.

Then Maya quietly grabbed paper towels and said:

"It's fine. That could've happened to literally anybody."

The tension disappeared almost instantly.

Liam smiled again.

People relaxed.

And within seconds, the group moved on completely.

What Maya did seemed small.
But emotionally, it changed everything.
Because one calm reaction can stop embarrassment from turning into humiliation.

Try This

The next time someone makes a mistake around you, notice your first reaction.

Do you make the moment heavier... or safer?

Do people around you become more tense... or more relaxed?

The people others trust most are often not the coolest people in the room.

They are the people who make everyone else feel less afraid of being human.

Saying Sorry So People Believe You

"Sorry."
Jordan said it fast.
Too fast.
Then he rolled his eyes and looked annoyed the entire time.

Nobody believed him.
Because apologies are not only made with words.
They are made with tone. Expression. Energy.
And people notice when those things do not match.

A real apology usually feels honest.
Not perfect.
Not dramatic.
Just real.

That's because humans constantly look for emotional consistency.

Your brain asks questions like:

- Does this person actually mean it?
- Do they understand the impact?
- Do their actions match their words?
- Does the apology feel defensive or sincere?

Sometimes people say "sorry" only because they want the problem to disappear quickly. Not because they truly understand what hurt someone.

And usually...
other people can feel that difference almost immediately.

Fake apologies often sound:

- rushed
- irritated
- sarcastic
- forced
- emotionless
- defensive

Real apologies usually contain responsibility. Not excuses.

They do not focus only on escaping consequences.
They focus on repairing trust.

Signals to Notice

- eye contact feels genuine instead of forced
- the tone sounds calm and sincere
- the person does not instantly blame others
- their body language looks open instead of defensive
- they care about the other person's feelings
- their behavior changes afterward
- the apology feels emotionally consistent

Words matter.
But behavior is what
makes people believe the words.

Real-Life Example

During group work, Ava accidentally deleted part of Mia's project slides.

At first, Ava panicked and said:

"Well, you should've saved it better."

Immediately, the room became tense.

A few minutes later, Ava walked back over quietly and said:

"Okay... that was my fault. I'm sorry. I know you worked really hard on that."

This time, her voice sounded different.
No excuses.
No attitude.

And without even realizing it, Mia relaxed almost immediately.

Because honest accountability often feels calming.

Try This

The next time you apologize to someone, pay attention to more than the words.

Notice your tone.

Your face.

Your energy.

Are you trying to understand the other person...
or just escape the uncomfortable moment quickly?

People usually forgive mistakes more easily than fake sincerity.

But when an apology feels real...
most people can feel that too.

Telling the Truth Clearly

"I mean... technically I didn't lie."

Ethan crossed his arms and stared at the floor.

"But I didn't exactly tell them either."

The room felt confusing after that.

Because everyone could sense the same thing: he was hiding behind words instead of speaking honestly.

A lot of people think truth is only about facts. But communication is also about clarity.

Sometimes a person avoids lying directly... while still trying to hide the real message.

- They speak vaguely.
- Change details.
- Leave important things out.
- Or answer questions in ways designed to escape responsibility.

And usually... people can feel that something is off.

That's because humans react strongly to mixed signals. When words feel slippery or unclear, trust becomes weaker.

Not always because the person is evil.

Sometimes people avoid clear honesty because they are:

- embarrassed
- scared of consequences
- trying to protect themselves
- afraid of disappointing someone
- nervous about conflict

But unclear truth often creates bigger problems later. Because confusion spreads uncertainty through the whole group.

One hidden social skill is learning how to speak honestly without hiding behind confusing language.

Clear communication usually sounds calmer and simpler than people expect.

When a person avoids clear honesty, they create distance — even if they think they are protecting themselves.

Truth told clearly is not always easy. But it builds trust faster than any other communication skill.

Honesty does not mean being harsh or blunt. It means being clear enough that people understand where you stand.

Signals to Notice

- answers feel overly complicated
- someone avoids the actual question
- details keep changing slightly
- the tone sounds defensive
- body language looks tense while speaking
- the explanation feels carefully controlled
- the words technically make sense... but still feel incomplete

Honest communication usually feels steady. Not slippery.

Real-Life Example

During class, a marker drawing appeared on the back wall near Noah's desk.

The teacher asked if anyone knew what happened.

Noah immediately said:

“Well... I wasn't the one holding the marker.”

Technically true.
But everybody noticed he avoided answering the real question.

A minute later, Noah sighed and admitted:

“Okay. I handed the marker to Tyler even though I knew what he was doing.”

The energy in the room changed instantly.

Not because the situation became perfect.

Because the truth finally became clear.

People relax faster when they know what is real.

Try This

The next time you explain something difficult, notice this:

Are you trying to communicate clearly...
or trying to escape discomfort?

Sometimes honesty feels scary for a few eeconds.

But unclear communication often creates tension that lasts much longer.

People may not always like the truth immediately...

but clear honesty usually builds more trust than confusing half-truths ever will.

Clear words.
Calm tone.
Steady honesty.
That's how trust grows.

Making Your Words, Voice, and Actions Match

Sophia said the words correctly.
But her voice sounded flat.
Her smile disappeared too quickly.
And she immediately changed the subject afterward.
Liam felt confused almost instantly.
Because even though the words sounded positive...
something underneath them did not match.

Humans trust consistency.

When words, tone, and behavior all point in the same direction, communication feels clear.
Safe.
Real.
But when those signals fight each other...
people feel uncertainty.

That's because your brain is constantly comparing different kinds of information at the same time:

the words

the voice

the face

the body language

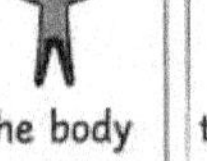

the emotional energy

And usually...
the emotional signals feel stronger than the words alone.

Someone can say:

"I'm fine."
while sounding hurt.

Or say:
"I was joking."
while looking angry.

Or say:
"I'm listening."
while staring at their phone.

When signals do not match, trust becomes weaker.

Not always because the person is lying.
Sometimes they are confused themselves.

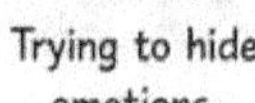

Trying to hide emotions.

Trying to sound nicer than they feel.

Or struggling to express what is really happening inside them.

But strong communicators learn something important:

clarity creates trust.

And clarity happens when your words, voice, and actions tell the same story.

Signals to Notice

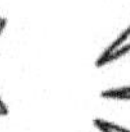

- the voice does not match the words
- facial expressions disappear too quickly
- body language feels closed while words sound friendly
- someone says one thing but behaves differently afterward
- the emotional energy feels inconsistent
- people look confused after the interaction
- trust feels weaker even without obvious conflict

Consistency feels emotionally safer than mixed signals.

Real-Life Example

During soccer tryouts, Coach Daniels told the team:

"Good effort today."

But everybody noticed something strange.

- ✕ He never looked up from his clipboard.
- ✕ His tone sounded distracted.
- ✕ And he walked away immediately after speaking.

The players looked at each other uncertainly.

Then Assistant Coach Rivera stepped forward smiling and said:

"You guys improved a lot today. Seriously. The passing looked way sharper."

This time, the energy felt different instantly.

Because his expression, voice, and body language all matched the message.

And suddenly, people actually believed it.

Try This

The next time you talk to someone, pay attention to this:

Do your words match your tone?

Does your body language support what you are saying?

If someone watched the interaction with the sound turned off... would they still understand the real message?

The strongest communicators are not the people with the fanciest words. They are the people whose signals all move in the same direction.

PART VIII

TRY THIS IN REAL LIFE

Understanding people is not something you learn only by reading about it.
You learn it by noticing things in real life.
Tiny moments.
Tiny reactions.
Tiny emotional patterns happening around you every single day.

That is why this section is different.
Instead of only explaining social signals...
you are going to practice spotting them yourself.

Because once you start observing people more carefully, something strange happens: you begin noticing things you never saw before.

- ★ A fake smile that disappears too quickly.
- ★ A nervous laugh.
- ★ Someone pretending to feel confident.
- ★ A group silently following one person's energy.
- ★ A calm person changing the mood of the room without saying much at all.

And suddenly...

 movies feel different.

 classrooms feel different.

 friendships feel different.

Because you start seeing the hidden emotional layer underneath conversations.
Not in a weird "reading minds" way.
More like becoming aware of signals your brain was already noticing unconsciously.

This section will challenge you to:

- observe people more carefully
- notice emotional patterns
- compare words with body language
- recognize real vs. fake reactions
- become aware of the signals you send too

Some activities may feel awkward at first.

- → Watching conversations without sound.
- → Studying facial expressions in a mirror.
- → Trying to guess emotions before somebody says them directly.

But that awkwardness is part of learning awareness.
Most people never practice these skills intentionally.
They simply move through social situations reacting automatically.
This section helps slow things down.

So you can finally notice:

- what changes the mood of a room
- why some people feel trustworthy instantly
- how tension quietly builds in groups
- how emotions spread between people
- how body language changes conversations

One important thing to remember:
the goal is not to judge people.
And it is definitely not to become obsessed with analyzing everybody around you.

Real social intelligence should make you more understanding... not more critical.

Because once you realize how many invisible emotions people carry every day...
you start seeing others with more empathy too.

You realize:
sometimes people act strange because they are nervous.

Sometimes they become loud because they feel insecure.

Sometimes they joke because they feel uncomfortable.

And sometimes people simply want to feel accepted like everybody else.

This section is about practicing awareness in the real world.

Because social intelligence is not a school subject most people ever get taught directly.
But once you begin noticing the hidden signals underneath human behavior...
you never see conversations the same way again.

Practice. Observe. Reflect. Grow.
That is how you unlock the secret language people use every single day.

The No-Word Challenge

Jake looked around the room, confused.
Nobody answered.
But somehow...
everybody already knew exactly what was happening.

One kid looked annoyed.

Another seemed nervous.

Two friends silently exchanged a look across the table.

Humans communicate constantly.
Even in silence.

And without using a single word, the entire mood of the room had changed.

In fact, people often reveal more through:

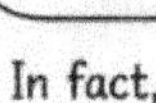

- facial expressions
- posture
- eye contact
- movement
- emotional energy

than through actual sentences.

That is why the "No-Word Challenge" can feel so strange at first.

The moment words disappear...
you suddenly notice how much communication was happening underneath them the whole time.

A nervous smile.	A fake laugh.	Someone leaning away from another person.	Someone trying to impress the group.	Someone feeling left out.

Your brain notices these signals automatically every day.
Most people just never slow down enough to consciously see them.

Signals to Notice

- ★ who gets interrupted without words
- ★ who people naturally look at most
- ★ who seems relaxed vs. tense
- ★ who copies other people's energy
- ★ who feels included
- ★ who looks uncomfortable
- ★ who controls the emotional mood of the group
- ★ how fast the room changes emotionally

Sometimes silence makes hidden social signals easier to notice.

Real-Life Example

During lunch, Emma challenged her friends:

"Okay. For one minute, nobody talks."

At first, everybody laughed. Then things got interesting.

Without words, people started noticing tiny details.

- ★ Who kept looking for approval.
- ★ Who avoided eye contact.
- ★ Who naturally became the center of attention.

One friend looked confident while talking normally... but seemed nervous the second words disappeared.

And another quiet student suddenly seemed much more emotionally aware than everyone expected.

When the minute ended, the whole group started talking at once.
Because for the first time, they had actually noticed how loud body language could be.

Try This

Today, spend one minute in a group conversation silently observing instead of talking.

Watch:

- faces
- posture
- reactions
- energy shifts
- eye contact

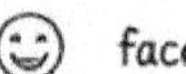

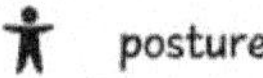

- ★ Notice who seems comfortable.
- ★ Notice who seems performative.
- ★ Notice who changes the emotional atmosphere of the room.

The hidden social world becomes much easier to understand... once you realize words are only part of the conversation.

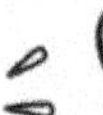

Watch a Movie With the Sound Off

At first, it felt impossible.
"How are we supposed to understand anything without sound?"

But after five minutes, Noah started noticing things he had never paid attention to before.

One character smiled...
while secretly looking angry.

Another kept leaning away during conversations.

A girl crossed her arms every time a certain person entered the room.

And somehow...
the emotions still made perfect sense even without hearing a single word.

Sometimes the most honest part of a conversation is happening silently in the background.

Most people think communication mainly happens through talking.

But movies reveal something important: humans constantly communicate visually.

Directors know this.

Actors know this.

Your brain knows this too.

That is why you can often tell:

- who feels awkward
- who is nervous
- who is lying
- who feels powerful
- who likes someone
- who feels left out

before anybody explains it out loud.

Body language changes the meaning of almost every scene.

A calm voice with crossed arms feels different than a calm voice with relaxed posture.

A smile with warm eyes feels different than a smile with tension underneath it.

Signals to Notice

- fake smiles
- eye rolls
- nervous fidgeting
- leaning toward or away from people
- forced laughter
- tension in shoulders or posture
- who people look at most often
- who controls the emotional mood of scenes
- moments where body language contradicts the words

Once you start noticing these signals...
movies almost become easier to "read."

Real-Life Example

During a sleepover, Mia and her cousins muted a movie during an argument scene just for fun.

At first, everyone laughed.

But then something surprising happened.

Without hearing the dialogue, they still understood almost everything.

One actor kept avoiding eye contact.

Another pointed aggressively while pretending to stay calm.

A third character looked uncomfortable long before speaking.

When the sound came back on, Mia realized something weird:

the words explained the story...
but the body language explained the emotions.

Try This

Tonight, watch five minutes of a movie or TV show with the sound completely off.

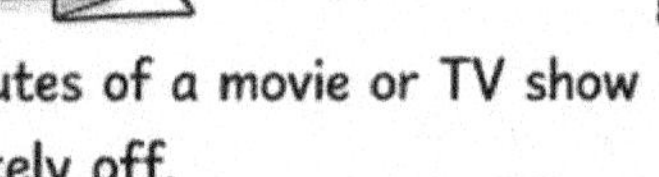

Then ask yourself:

- Who seems confident?
- Who seems uncomfortable?
- Who has power in the scene?
- Who is trying to hide emotions?
- Which relationships feel genuine?

You will probably notice something surprising:

people reveal far more through expressions, posture, and energy... than most words ever say directly.

Guess the Real Emotion

"Guess how she feels."

Maya paused the video right in the middle of the scene.

The girl on screen was smiling.

So everyone said:

"Happy."

But Maya shook her head.

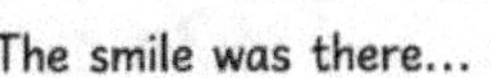

"Look closer."

The smile was there...

but her shoulders were tight.

Her eyes looked shiny.

And her hands were gripping her backpack straps like she wanted to disappear.

Suddenly, the answer changed.

She was not happy.
She was <u>trying</u> to look happy.

That is the secret behind real emotions: **they do not always match the obvious expression.**

 People sometimes smile when they are nervous.

 Laugh when they are embarrassed.

 Say "it's fine" when they feel hurt.

 Act annoyed when they are actually scared.

Your job is not to guess perfectly. Nobody can do that all the time.

↓

The skill is learning to notice when the first answer might not be the full answer.

Signals to Notice

- the face says one thing, but the body says another
- the smile disappears too quickly
- the person looks away at emotional moments
- their voice becomes smaller or sharper
- their hands seem tense
- their posture closes up
- their energy changes after one comment

Real emotions often hide in the tiny details.

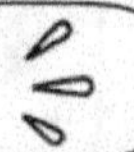

Real-Life Example

During lunch, Ava said she was excited about the group project.

She smiled.

She nodded.

She even said:

"Yeah, sounds fun."

But when the group started assigning parts, Ava became quieter.

She stopped making eye contact.

And every time someone mentioned presenting in front of the class...

...she touched her necklace and looked down.

"She's <u>not</u> excited," he thought. "She's nervous."

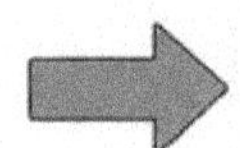

And he was right.

Try This

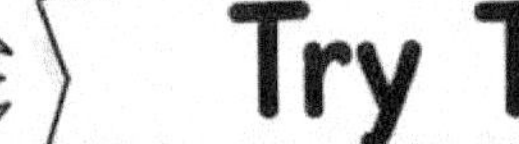

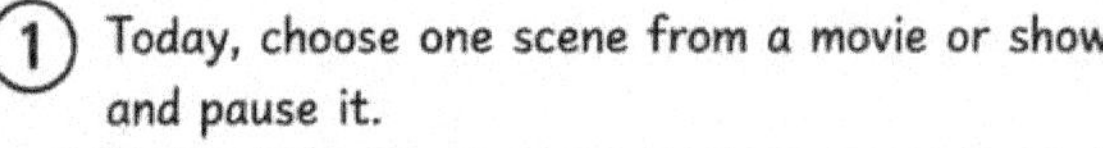

1. Today, choose one scene from a movie or show and pause it.

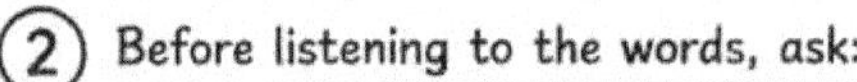

2. Before listening to the words, ask:

   "What emotion is this person trying to show?"

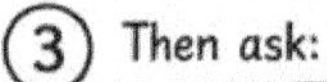

3. Then ask:

   "What emotion might they actually be feeling?"

The more you practice, the easier it becomes to see the difference between the <u>mask</u>... and the <u>real feeling</u> underneath.

The Mirror Exercise

"Wait... I actually do that?"

- ★ Jordan stared at his reflection for a second longer than usual.
- ★ He had never noticed how nervous he looked during conversations.
- ★ The quick fake smile.
- ★ The way he crossed his arms.
- ★ The way he looked away too fast when someone made eye contact.

Most people have no idea what signals they send to other people.
Because you cannot fully see your own expressions while you are making them.

That is why the mirror exercise feels strange at first.
But also powerful.

The goal is not to become fake or overly controlled.
It is not about "performing."
It is about becoming aware.

Because once you notice your own signals... you start understanding other people's signals better too.

Humans constantly communicate through tiny reactions:

- facial tension
- posture
- eye contact
- nervous habits
- energy shifts
- tone changes

And many of those reactions happen automatically.

The mirror exercise helps bring some of those invisible habits into awareness.

Signals to Notice

- ✓ fake smiles that disappear quickly
- ✓ nervous laughter
- ✓ avoiding eye contact immediately
- ✓ tense shoulders
- ✓ crossing arms when uncomfortable
- ✓ forced "confident" expressions
- ✓ fidgeting without realizing it
- ✓ expressions changing before words do

Sometimes your face reveals emotions before your brain catches up.

Real-Life Example

Before a class presentation, Emma practiced in front of the mirror at home.

At first, she focused only on the words. But then she noticed something surprising.

Every time she felt unsure, she pressed her lips together tightly.

Every time she forgot part of the presentation, her shoulders lifted toward her ears.

And when she forced herself to "look confident," she accidentally looked angry instead.

The next day, Emma relaxed her shoulders, slowed down her breathing, and softened her expression during the presentation.

Nothing became perfect.
But she looked calmer...
because she actually felt calmer too.

Try This

Stand in front of a mirror for one minute and try saying:

"I'm fine."

"I'm excited."

"I don't care."

"I'm sorry."

Then ask yourself:

Would somebody believe me only from my face and tone?

Or do my signals say something different underneath?

The better you understand your own signals...
the easier it becomes to understand everyone else's too.

Reading Text Messages Like a Detective

"Okay."
That was the entire reply.
Just one word.
No emoji. No exclamation point.
No extra sentence.
And somehow...
Sophie immediately started wondering if her friend was upset.

Text messages are strange because they remove huge parts of communication.

You cannot hear the voice.

See the face.

Or feel the energy in the room.

So your brain starts searching for clues in tiny details instead.

Things like:

- punctuation
- response time
- emojis
- message length
- capitalization
- typing style

That is why:

can feel completely different from:

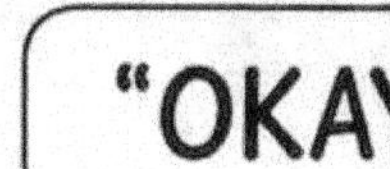

"OKAY!!! "

Even though the actual word is almost the same.

Humans naturally try to fill emotional gaps when information is missing.
Sometimes correctly.
Sometimes completely wrong.

That is one reason texting creates so many misunderstandings.

People often read emotions into messages that were never intended.
Especially when they already feel nervous, insecure, embarrassed, or left out.

Signals to Notice

- suddenly shorter replies than usual
- delayed responses
- missing emojis from someone who normally uses them
- extra punctuation that changes the emotional tone
- messages that feel unusually cold or rushed
- one-word answers during emotional conversations
- overthinking tiny wording differences

But remember:
one text message alone rarely tells the full story.
Patterns matter more than isolated moments.

Real-Life Example

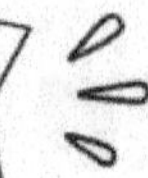

Late one night,
Ava texted her friend:

"Did I say something weird earlier?"

Her friend replied:

"No."

That was it.
No smiley face.
No "lol."
No extra explanation.

"She's definitely mad at me."

Immediately, Ava's stomach dropped.

The next day at school, Ava finally asked about it in person.

Her friend blinked in confusion. "What? No. I was literally half asleep when I answered."

Suddenly the whole situation felt completely different.

Because text messages often remove the emotional signals people normally use to understand each other clearly.

No voice.
No facial expression.
No tone.
No body language.

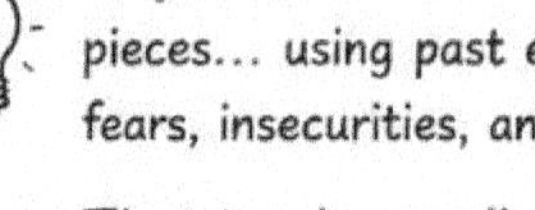

So your brain fills in the missing pieces... using past experiences, fears, insecurities, and assumptions.

That is why small messages can feel huge sometimes.

Try This

The next time a text message feels "cold" or confusing, pause before creating a whole story in your head.

Ask yourself:

- Am I reacting to facts... or guessing emotions?
- Is this a pattern... or one single message?
- Would this feel different if I heard their actual voice?

Sometimes the brain becomes a detective while texting.
The problem is...
detectives are not always right.

The Skill Most Adults Never Learn

Two people walked into the same room.
One left feeling respected.
The other left feeling invisible.

- ★ Nothing huge had happened.
- ★ No argument.
- ★ No dramatic moment.
- ★ Just tiny signals.
- ★ Tiny reactions.
- ★ Tiny emotional shifts most people never notice consciously.

But those invisible moments shape almost every friendship, group, classroom, and conversation in life.

That is the strange thing about communication: most people spend years learning math, grammar, history, and science...
without ever being taught how humans actually affect each other emotionally.

So people grow up confused.

- ▶ They misunderstand tone.
- ▶ Miss social signals.
- ▶ Assume the wrong things.
- ▶ Accidentally hurt people.
- ▶ Feel left out without understanding why.
- ▶ Or spend years believing something is "wrong" with them... when really nobody ever explained the hidden social rules underneath everyday life.

That is why emotional awareness
is such a powerful skill.
Not because it makes you perfect.
But because it helps you see more clearly.

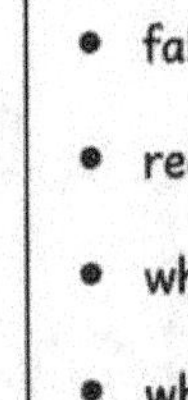

You start noticing:

- tension before conflict explodes
- discomfort before someone says anything
- fake confidence hiding insecurity
- real kindness hiding quietly in the background
- who makes people feel safe
- who changes the emotional direction of a group
- when words and emotions stop matching

And once you start seeing those signals...

people stop feeling quite so confusing.

Signals to Notice

- how people affect the emotional energy of a room
- who listens vs. who only waits to speak
- which people make others relax
- when body language contradicts words
- who changes depending on the group
- how groups quietly decide inclusion and exclusion
- the difference between attention and trust

The biggest social skill
is not manipulation.
It is awareness.

Real-Life Example

At the end of the school year, Mr. Bennett asked his students something simple:

"Who in this class makes people feel comfortable talking?"

The answers surprised everyone.
The loudest kids were not mentioned most.
Neither were the funniest.

Again and again, students named people who:

- ★ listened carefully
- ★ stayed calm during awkward moments
- ★ included quieter classmates
- ★ noticed when someone looked uncomfortable
- ★ treated people consistently

That was the moment many students realized something adults often miss completely:

the people others trust most are not always the people demanding attention.

Very often, they are the people who understand emotions best.

Try This

For one day, become a quiet observer of the emotional world around you.

Notice:

- who changes the mood of a room
- who makes people feel safer
- who listens well
- who performs constantly
- who seems lonely
- who quietly helps others relax

And notice yourself too.
How does your energy affect other people?

Because this skill is not really about "reading" humans like machines. It is about understanding that everybody around you is constantly sending signals...

hoping someone understands them.

Most adults never fully learn to notice those signals.

But now?
You can.

Social Signal Quiz

You walk into a room.
Someone looks at you for half a second...
then quickly looks away.

What does it mean?

Maybe nothing.
Maybe everything.

That's the tricky part about social signals.

Most people think communication is only about words.
But your brain is constantly reading:

- ★ faces
- ★ tone of voice
- ★ posture
- ★ eye contact
- ★ energy
- ★ silence

Sometimes you notice it instantly.

Sometimes you only feel it.

This quiz is designed to help you become a better social detective.

Not by overthinking people.
Not by judging them.
But by learning to notice the hidden signals most people miss.

HOW TO USE THIS QUIZ

For each situation:

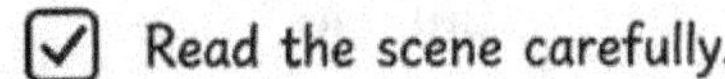

- ☑ Read the scene carefully.
- ☑ Look for the hidden social clues.
- ☑ Pick the answer that feels MOST likely.
- ☑ Don't worry about being perfect.

Real people are complicated.
But strong observers notice patterns.

**Ready?
Let's begin.**

1. THE FAST SMILE

You show your drawing to a classmate.
They smile very quickly and say:

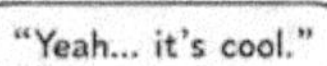

But the smile disappears almost immediately.

What signal might your brain notice?

A) They are super excited
B) Their words and feelings may not fully match
C) They didn't hear you
D) They are secretly angry

Answer:

Sometimes people say something positive... but their face disappears too fast.
Your brain notices tiny timing differences before you even understand them.

2. THE GROUP LAUGH

A group of kids is laughing together.
One kid laughs too... but keeps glancing around before laughing.

What might that mean?

A) They feel relaxed
B) They already heard the joke
C) They may be checking if it's "safe" to laugh
D) They are bored

Answer:

People often copy group behavior when they want to fit in.
Especially in groups.
Especially at school.

3. THE QUIET "OKAY"

A teacher says:

"That's interesting..."

But their voice sounds flat and tired.

What signal matters MOST here?

A) The exact word
B) The tone of voice
C) Their shoes
D) How loud the classroom is

Answer:

Words matter.
But tone changes meaning fast.
The same sentence can sound:

- excited
- annoyed
- sarcastic
- disappointed

depending on the voice behind it.

4. THE LUNCH TABLE SIGNAL

You sit down at a lunch table.
Nobody says "leave."
But nobody moves over either.

What hidden signal could this create?

A) You feel instantly relaxed
B) You feel welcomed
C) You may feel tolerated instead of included
D) Nothing important

Answer:

Sometimes exclusion is silent.
Nobody says anything directly.
But the energy changes anyway.

5. THE TOO-FAST JOKE

Someone teases another kid.
Then immediately says:

"Relax. I was kidding."

But the other kid stops talking completely.

What signal matters MOST?

A) The joke itself
B) The reaction afterward
C) The backpack color
D) The classroom noise

Answer:

People often reveal emotions after the moment happens.
Silence can be a signal too.

6. THE CONFIDENT PERSON

Two people are presenting in class.
One talks loudly and fast.
The other speaks calmly and slowly.
The room listens more carefully to the second person.
Why?

A) Calm energy can feel more confident
B) Loud always means leadership
C) Fast talking always sounds smarter
D) Confidence only comes from volume

Answer:

Real confidence is not always loud.
Sometimes calm people control the room without trying.

7. THE "I'M FINE" MOMENT

Your friend says:

"I'm fine."

But they avoid eye contact and answer very quickly.

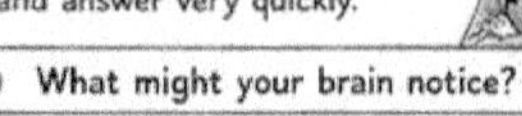

What might your brain notice?

A) Their words and body language don't fully match
B) They are definitely lying
C) Nothing important
D) They forgot something

Answer:

Not every mismatch means dishonesty.
Sometimes people hide feelings because they:

- feel embarrassed
- feel nervous
- don't want attention
- don't know how to explain themselves

FINAL SCORE

0-2 Correct
You're just starting to notice hidden social signals.
Most people never even begin.

3-5 Correct
Your brain already catches more than you realize.
You're becoming a stronger observer.

6-7 Correct
You notice patterns most people miss.
That's real social awareness.
Not mind-reading.
Observation.

ONE LAST THING

The goal is NOT to become suspicious of everyone.
The goal is to understand people better.

Because once you start noticing:

- tone
- timing
- expressions
- silence
- energy

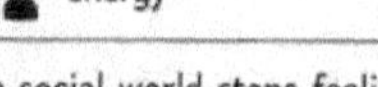

the social world stops feeling random.
And suddenly...
a lot more things make sense.

ANSWER KEY

YOUR BRAIN IS GETTING BETTER AT SEEING HIDDEN SIGNALS.

1. THE FAST SMILE

Answer:

Sometimes people say something positive...
but their face disappears too fast.
Your brain notices tiny timing differences before you even understand them.

2. THE GROUP LAUGH

Answer:

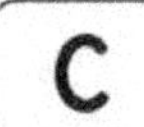

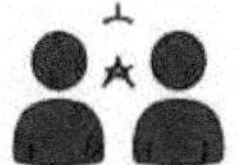

People often copy group behavior when they want to fit in.
Especially in groups.
Especially at school.

3. THE QUIET "OKAY"

Answer:

Words matter.
But tone changes meaning fast.
The same sentence can sound:

- excited
- annoyed
- sarcastic
- disappointed

depending on the voice behind it.

4. THE LUNCH TABLE SIGNAL

Answer:

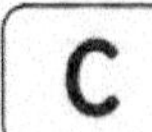

Sometimes exclusion is silent.
Nobody says anything directly.
But the energy changes anyway.

5. THE TOO-FAST JOKE

Answer:

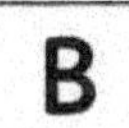

People often reveal emotions after the moment happens.
Silence can be a signal too.

6. THE CONFIDENT PERSON

Answer:

Real confidence is not always loud.
Sometimes calm people control the room without trying.

7. THE "I'M FINE" MOMENT

Answer:

Not every mismatch means dishonesty.
Sometimes people hide feelings because they:

- feel embarrassed
- feel nervous
- don't want attention
- don't know how to explain themselves

FINAL SCORE

0–2 Correct

You're just starting to notice hidden social signals.
Most people never even begin.

3–5 Correct

Your brain already catches more than you realize.
You're becoming a stronger observer.

6–7 Correct

You notice patterns most people miss.
That's real social awareness.
Not mind-reading.
Observation.

ONE LAST THING

The goal is NOT to become suspicious of everyone.
The goal is to understand people better.

Because once you start noticing:

- tone
- timing
- expressions
- silence
- energy

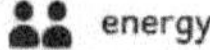

the social world stops feeling random.

And suddenly...
a lot more things make sense.

YOU DID IT! You just trained your brain to see what most people miss. | Keep noticing. Keep observing. Keep growing.

DECODE THE EXPRESSION GAME

Faces talk fast.
Sometimes before words even show up.
A kid says, "I'm not mad."
But their jaw is tight.
Someone says, "That's funny."
But their eyes don't smile.
A friend says, "Go ahead."
But their face looks like they wish you wouldn't.

This game helps you practice reading expressions without jumping to conclusions.
Because the goal is not to "catch" people.
The goal is to notice.

HOW TO PLAY

1. Look at each expression clue.
2. Ask yourself: What might this person be feeling?
3. Then choose the best answer.
4. There may be more than one possible emotion, but one answer fits the signals best.

1. THE FAST DISAPPEARING SMILE

A girl smiles when someone compliments her shirt.
But the smile disappears almost instantly.
Then she looks down.

What might she feel?

A) Proud and relaxed
B) Embarrassed or unsure
C) Angry
D) Bored

Answer:

Sometimes people like a compliment... but don't know what to do with it.
A fast smile can mean the feeling was real, but uncomfortable.

2. THE TIGHT JAW

A boy says, "It's fine."
But his jaw is tight, and he keeps pressing his lips together.

What signal should you notice?

A) He may be holding back frustration
B) He is probably sleepy
C) He is trying to be funny
D) He feels completely calm

Answer:

A tight jaw can be a clue that someone is trying not to react.
Not always.
But often enough to notice.

3. THE SMILE WITHOUT THE EYES

Someone laughs and smiles.
But their eyes stay still.

What might this mean?

A) The smile may be polite, not fully real
B) They are definitely happy
C) They are confused about math
D) They want to run

Answer:

Real smiles often reach the eyes.
Polite smiles sometimes stay only on the mouth.

4. THE RAISED EYEBROWS

A teacher looks at the class with raised eyebrows and a silent face.
Nobody is talking anymore.

What might that expression mean?

A) "I'm waiting."
B) "I'm very excited."
C) "I forgot where I am."
D) "This is hilarious."

Answer:

Some expressions don't need words.
Raised eyebrows plus silence can say:
"I noticed that. Now what are you going to do?"

5. THE FROZEN FACE

Your friend usually talks a lot.
Today, someone makes a joke about them.
They smile a little, but their face looks frozen.

What might be happening?

A) They loved the joke
B) They may feel hurt but don't want to show it
C) They didn't hear anything
D) They are planning lunch

Answer:

A frozen face can happen when someone is trying to stay cool on the outside.
Inside, something may have landed harder than people realize.

6. THE SIDE-EYE

Someone looks at another person from the side without turning their head.
Their mouth is flat.

What could this signal?

A) Suspicion, annoyance, or "Really?"
B) Pure happiness
C) Sleepiness
D) Total agreement

Answer:

Side-eye is often a quiet signal.
It can mean, "I saw that."
Or, "I don't believe this."

7. THE REAL SMILE

Someone sees their friend walk into the room.
Their face changes immediately.
Their eyes brighten.
Their shoulders relax.

What is the strongest clue?

A) Their whole body changed
B) They blinked once
C) They had shoes on
D) They stood near a desk

Answer:

Real feelings often show up in more than one place. Face. Eyes. Shoulders. Energy.
That's when the signal gets stronger.

FINAL RULE OF THE GAME

Never decide someone's whole story from one expression.

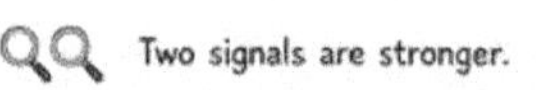

One signal is a clue.

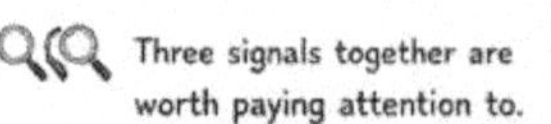

Two signals are stronger.

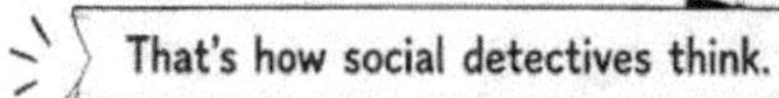

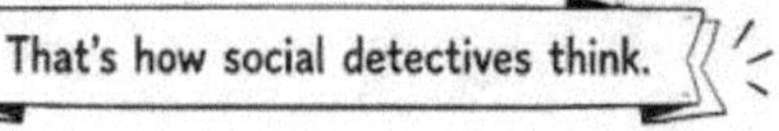

Three signals together are worth paying attention to.

That's how social detectives think.

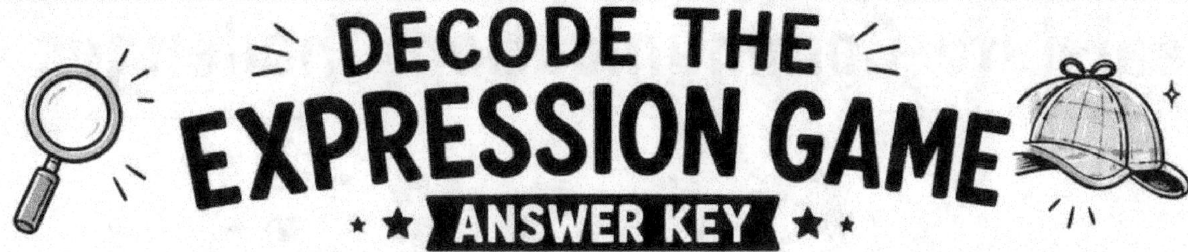

DECODE THE EXPRESSION GAME

ANSWER KEY

Great job, detective!
You practiced noticing the tiny clues people show before they speak. Keep observing. You're getting better every time you notice.

1 THE FAST DISAPREARING SMILE

A girl smiles when someone compliments her shirt. But the smile disappears almost instantly. Then she looks down.

Best Answer: 

Sometimes people like a compliment... but don't know what to do with it. A fast smile can mean the feeling was real, but uncomfortable.

2 THE TIGHT JAW

A boy says, "It's fine." But his jaw is tight, and he keeps pressing his lips together.

Best Answer: 

A tight jaw can be a clue that someone is trying not to react. Not always. But often enough to notice.

3 THE SMILE WITHOUT THE EYES

Someone laughs and smiles. But their eyes stay still.

Best Answer: 

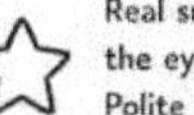

Real smiles often reach the eyes. Polite smiles sometimes stay only on the mouth.

4 THE RAISED EYEBROWS

A teacher looks at the class with raised eyebrows and a silent face. Nobody is talking anymore.

Best Answer: 

Some expressions don't need words. Raised eyebrows plus silence can say: "I noticed that. Now what are you going to do?"

5 THE FROZEN FACE

Your friend usually talks a lot. Today, someone makes a joke about them. They smile a little, but their face looks frozen.

Best Answer: 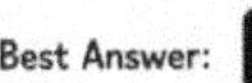

A frozen face can happen when someone is trying to stay cool on the outside. Inside, something may have landed harder than people realize.

6 THE SIDE-EYE

Someone looks at another person from the side without turning their head. Their mouth is flat.

Best Answer: 

Side-eye is often a quiet signal. It can mean, "I saw that." Or, "I don't believe this."

7 THE REAL SMILE

Someone sees their friend walk into the room. Their face changes immediately. Their eyes brighten. Their shoulders relax.

Best Answer: A

Real feelings often show up in more than one place. Face. Eyes. Shoulders. Energy. That's when the signal gets stronger.

FINAL RULE OF THE GAME

★ Never decide someone's whole story from one expression.

★ One signal is a clue.

★★ Two signals are stronger.

★★★ Three signals together are worth paying attention to.

That's how social detectives think.

You're building a skill most people never practice. Keep going, detective!

Real-Life Communication Challenges

Sometimes the hardest social moments happen fast.
Too fast.
A weird silence. A fake laugh.
A group suddenly going quiet.
Someone saying "whatever" in a voice that definitely does not mean "whatever."
This section is different.
There are no perfect answers.
Because real people are messy.
But strong observers notice patterns before things fully explode.

YOUR JOB:

 Read the situation.

 Look for the hidden signals.

 Then decide what you would do.

❶ The Group Chat Freeze

You send a joke in the group chat.
Nobody answers.
Five minutes pass.
Then someone changes the subject completely.

Silence online can feel loud. Especially when the conversation suddenly moves around you instead of through you. That does NOT always mean people hate you. But your brain notices the shift immediately.

What signal might this create?

A) The joke may not have landed well
B) Everyone suddenly fell asleep
C) Phones stopped working
D) Nothing happened

Best Answer: ______

Better Response:
Instead of panicking or sending:
"Wow okay"
ignore me then."
Just let the conversation move.
Confident people do not chase every reaction.

❷ The Weird Laugh

A kid keeps teasing another student.
Everyone laughs.
But one person's laugh sounds forced.
They stop laughing before everyone else.

What hidden signal matters MOST?

A) The joke was funny
B) Someone may feel uncomfortable
C) Everybody enjoyed it
D) The room feels relaxed

Best Answer: ______

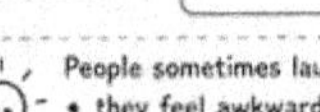

People sometimes laugh because:
- they feel awkward
- they want to fit in
- they don't want attention on themselves

Not every laugh means enjoyment.

❸ The Teacher Voice

The classroom gets noisy.
Your teacher says:
"Guys."
Very quietly.
And suddenly everybody stops talking.

Why?

A) Quiet voices can carry authority
B) Loudness always controls people
C) Everyone got tired
D) The lights changed

Best Answer: ______

Calm voices can feel more powerful than shouting.
Especially when the room senses real control underneath the calm.

❹ The Lunch Table Problem

You walk toward a lunch table.
People are talking normally.
Then the energy changes slightly when you arrive.
Nobody says anything rude.
But nobody makes space either.

Some social moments are invisible. That's why they feel confusing. Nobody explains what happened. But your brain still feels it.

What challenge are you facing?

A) Reading a silent social signal
B) A math problem
C) A classroom rule
D) A joke contest

Best Answer: ______

Try This:
Instead of freezing:
- stay calm
- notice the energy
- choose confidently

Sometimes the strongest move is acting comfortable instead of panicked.

❺ "I'm Fine"

Your friend says:
"I'm fine."
But:
- their voice is flat
- they avoid eye contact
- their answers become shorter

What is the BEST response?

A) "You're obviously lying."
B) Ignore them completely
C) "You seem quieter than usual."
D) "Why are you acting weird?"

Best Answer: ______

Strong communicators notice signals without attacking people.
That creates safety.
And safety makes people open up more.

❻ The Reaction Trap

Someone keeps trying to annoy you in front of other people.
They smirk every time you react.

What might they actually want?

A) Entertainment and control
B) Homework help
C) Friendship advice
D) Silence

Best Answer: ______

Some people test reactions because reactions create power.
The bigger your reaction becomes... the more control they feel.

Strong Move:
Slow down.
Pause before reacting.
Calm people are harder to control.

❼ The Invisible Leader

In a group project,
one student barely talks.
But when they finally speak...
everyone listens.
Why?

A) Leadership is not always loud
B) Quiet people never matter
C) Loudness equals respect
D) People are confused

Best Answer: ______

Real social influence is often quieter than people expect.
Sometimes the calmest person changes the entire room.

 FINAL CHALLENGE — THE MOST IMPORTANT SIGNAL

What is the BIGGEST mistake people make when reading others?

A) Watching only words
B) Noticing tone
C) Paying attention to expressions
D) Observing behavior patterns

Best Answer: ______

Words matter.
But people also communicate through:
- timing
- silence
- posture
- tone
- facial expressions
- energy changes

That's the hidden world most people never learn to see.
Until now.

REAL-LIFE COMMUNICATION CHALLENGES

ANSWER KEY

Great job, detective! You spotted the hidden signals and thought about what to do. That's how strong observers grow.

1 THE GROUP CHAT FREEZE

Best Answer:

Silence online can feel loud.
Especially when the conversation suddenly moves around you instead of through you.

Better Response:

Instead of panicking or sending:
"Wow okay ignore me then."
Just let the conversation move.
Confident people do not chase every reaction.

2 THE WEIRD LAUGH

Best Answer:

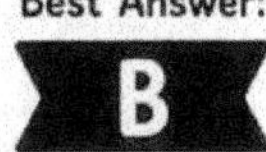

People sometimes laugh because:

- they feel awkward
- they want to fit in
- they don't want attention on themselves

Not every laugh means enjoyment.

3 THE TEACHER VOICE

Best Answer:

Calm voices can feel more powerful than shouting.
Especially when the room senses real control underneath the calm.

4 THE LUNCH TABLE PROBLEM

Best Answer:

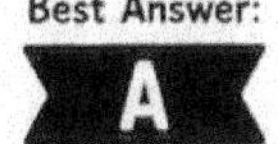

Some social moments are invisible.
That's why they feel confusing.
Nobody explains what happened.
But your brain still feels it.

Try This:

- stay calm
- notice the energy
- choose confidently

Sometimes the strongest move is acting comfortable instead of panicked.

5 "I'M FINE"

Best Answer:

Strong communicators notice signals without attacking people.
That creates safety.
And safety makes people open up more.

6 THE REACTION TRAP

Best Answer:

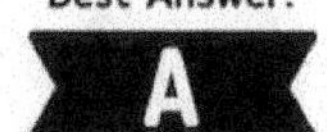

Some people test reactions because reactions create power.
The bigger your reaction becomes...
the more control they feel.

Strong Move:

Slow down. Pause before reacting.
Calm people are harder to control.

7 THE INVISIBLE LEADER

Best Answer:

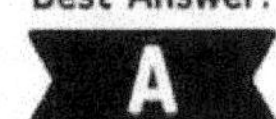

Real social influence is often quieter than people expect.
Sometimes the calmest person changes the entire room.

FINAL CHALLENGE — THE MOST IMPORTANT SIGNAL

Best Answer:

But people also communicate through:

- timing
- silence
- posture
- tone
- facial expressions
- energy changes

That's the hidden world most people never learn to see.
Until now.

You don't need perfect answers.
You need attention, curiosity, and a calm mind.

Keep observing. Keep learning.
Keep growing.

REMEMBER:

- ★ People send signals all the time.
- ★ Most signals are small and fast.
- ★ Strong observers notice patterns.
- ★ Your response shapes the moment.
- ★ Calm confidence is your superpower.

CERTIFICATE
OF
OBSERVATION SKILLS

This certifies that

____

has successfully completed

The Mehrabian Rule for Kids

and has learned how to:

✓ Notice hidden social signals
✓ Read tone, facial expressions, and body language
✓ Understand when words and feelings do not match
✓ Observe group energy and social dynamics
✓ Communicate with more confidence and awareness
✓ Think like a real social detective

SPECIAL SKILLS UNLOCKED

- Spotting fake confidence
- Reading the mood of a room
- Listening beyond words
- Staying calm under social pressure
- Understanding the invisible rules people never explain

OFFICIAL TITLE EARNED:

☆ ☆ ☆ ☆ ☆

SOCIAL SIGNAL DETECTIVE

☆ ☆ ☆ ☆

DATE COMPLETED: ____________________

SIGNATURE: ____________________

FINAL REMINDER

The strongest observers are not the loudest people.
They are the people who notice:

- expressions
- silence
- timing
- tone
- energy

...and understand what those signals might mean.

Keep noticing.
Most people never do.

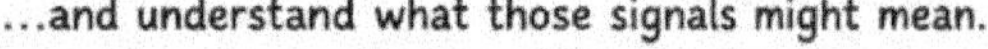

www.ingramcontent.com/pod-product-compliance
Lightning Source LLC
LaVergne TN
LVHW061204120826
845149LV00011B/1901
* 9 7 8 1 9 5 6 2 8 9 5 2 7 *